New Propulsion System

No part of this publication may be reproduced stored in a retrieval system or transmitted in any form or by any means electronic, mechanical, photocopying, recording, scanning, or otherwise, except as permitted under Sections 107 or 108 of the United States Copyright act, without prior written permission of the Author.

LIMIT OF LIABLILITY/DISCLAIMER OF WARRANTY: THE PUBLISHER AND THE AUTHOR MAKES NO REPRESENTATIONS OR WARRANTIES WITH RESPECT TO THE ACCURACY OR COMPLETENESS OF THE CONTENTS OF THIS WORK AND SPECIFICALLY DISCLAIM ALL WARRANTIES, INCLUDING WITHOUT LIMITATION WARRANTIES OF FITNESS FOR A PARTICULAR PURPOSE. NO WARRANTY MAY BE CREATED OR EXTENDED BY SALES OR PROMOTIONAL MATERIALS. THE ADVICE AND STATEGIES CONTAINED HEREIN MAY NOT BE SUITABLE FOR EVERY SITUATION. THIS WORK IS SOLD WITH THE UNDERSTANDING THAT THE PUBLISHER IS NOT ENGAGED IN RENDERING LEGAL, ACCOUNTING, OR OTHER PROFESSIONAL SERVICES. IF PROFESSIONAL ASSISTANCE IS REQUIRED, THE SERVICES OF COMPETENT PROFESSIONAL PERSON SHOULD BE SOUGHT. NEITHER THE PUBLISHER NOR THE AUTHOR SHALL BE LIABLE FOR DAMAGES ARISING HEREFROM. THE FACT THAT AN ORGANIZATION OR WEBSITE IS REFFERED TO IN THIS WORK AS A CITATION AND/OR A POTENTIAL SOURCE OF FURTHER INFORMATION DOES NOT MEAN THAT THE AUTHOR OR THE PUBLISHER ENDORSES THE INFORMATION THE ORGANIZATION OR WEBSITE MAY PROVIDE OR RECOMMENDATIONS IT MAKE MAKE. FURTHER, READERS SHOULD BE AWARE THAT INTERNET WEBSITES LISTED IN THIS WORK MAY HAVE CHANGED OR DISAPPEARED BETWEEN WHEN THIS WORK WAS WRITTEN AND WHEN IT IS READ.

New propulsion system

Don't forget to visit the website blog for updates and detail engineering drawings

https://davedelgado.webs.com/

Table of Contents

New propulsion system

New propulsion system

Introduction

The primary purpose of this book is education - for the student, the designer, and the individual whose interest and the aim is to design and build his propulsion system using steam energy. The material selected for the presentation has been carefully prepared to give the reader a basic understanding of the requirements for the new steam-power propulsion design.

Ralph Waldo Emerson said, *"**Build a better mousetrap and the world will beat a path to your door.**"* It is hoped that the following innovative design concept will be that mousetrap.

The propulsion system used in this book includes a powerful two-cylinder cross-compound reciprocating engine similar to the Stanley Motor Carriage engines. Also, heat exchangers were sized using NASA (TN D-5813) method of calculations for a hypothetical 4000 lb vehicle load with a 175 hp (290 hp) engine. The design trend was to provide an affordable and producible system with easy to build features with common parts and materials. An F150-F250 Ford pickup chassis with rear-wheel differential was selected for system integration.

Individuals contemplating a steam-power "design-build" project should consider devoting ample time to familiarize themselves with the basic fundamental of the Rankine Cycle, the basics in thermodynamics and their laws. These areas of study are recommended as the basic criteria with which to become fully acquainted. Application of theory, principals and processes are the major factors involved. Therefore, the individual must learn to analyze problems and apply the fundamentals. It is hoped that the individual may be stimulated to pursue and obtain technical literature available elsewhere.

The best and most fun way to get educated about steam is to attend a steam engine show. There are almost 5,000 steam engine shows across the nation. Steam has its fraternity of dedicated individuals. Many like to restore old machines and show them off.

It is my sincere hope and desire that this text will help if only in a minute way, to stimulate the student or "design-build" enthusiast to emerge with even one facet of design improvement and simplification which will add its impact to progress in steam-power design.

New propulsion system

You are probably aware that the steam automobile is not new. Maybe you have seen Jay Leno driving some of his steam cars around in Southern California. The late Ted Pritchard converted 1963 Ford Falcon to steam power in Australia. In November 1972 the car was flown to LA for demonstrations to big motor companies. They were quite impressed with the small car with green stripes. Billionaire, Howard Hughes "tooled" around with steam-powered cars and a couple of years back, a 1963 Volkswagen Beetle was converted to steam power by the nuclear scientist.

The development cost for any steam-power conversion project may sore. Ted Pritchard said his cost was $150,000 (1970 dollars). Billionaire, Howard Hughes had to abandon his steam car project. The automobile industry invested millions of man-hours and over billions of dollars to develop their Internal Ccombustion engines. The key to success is found in Producibility, Engineering, and Planning (PEP).

PEP covers strength, reliability, thermal considerations, corrosion, wear, friction, cost, safety, weight, noise, styling shape, size, stiffness, and types of lubrication.

The cost of materials and labor will vary from place to place. Therefore, nothing can be said in an absolute sense concerning cost. However, the cost is expected to be substantially lower than the typical internal combustion engine rebuilt costs. Furthermore, to keep the cost down, the design concept embraced standard sizes and large tolerances.

What is new in this book is the two-cylinder cross-compound double-acting reciprocating engine using common parts and material that is easily integrated onto a Ford chassis with a rear differential as a new propulsion alternative to the internal combustion engine. The engine shall provide more power, better reliability with fewer moving parts, compact size, quieter with no explosions, less vibration and zero-carbon admissions. In other words, No pollution.

New propulsion system

For reference, the labor leader in the House of Commons on July 17, 2019, said in questions to the prime minister, every year 40,000 people in his country die from air pollution. He said the government won't meet their net-zero admissions target until 2099. Roughly, 3.2 million deaths later. Sad but true from a country where steam energy helped fuel the industrial revolution.

To begin with, the majority of the new propulsion system is already complete. Such as a vehicle with headlights, air conditioning, heater, radio, windshield wipers, passenger cab, seats, rear differential drive, propeller shaft, electrical fuses, wiring harnesses, power steering with pump, radiator with fans, alternator, power windows, and a chassis frame.

The junkyard may be a good place to start. However, you may want to drop the internal-combustion engine, transmission, catalytic converter, mufflers, and gasoline tank.

All materials required for the two-cylinder cross-compound double-acting reciprocating engine may be picked up from a local metal supply company and a plumbers supply house. For the total propulsion system, McMaster Carr and local auto supply stores may be added to the list.

Engine installation includes securing the engine to the chassis with 4 mounting fasteners. Connecting the engine drive shaft to the propeller shaft. Connecting input and exhaust pipes and attaching the reverse link threaded rod to the reverse lever threaded clevis mounted on the floor in the passenger cab. That is it. You have installed a powerful engine in less time it takes to replace a water pump on a typical internal combustion engine.

The total propulsion system includes the two-cylinder cross-compound double-acting reciprocating engine, a boiler burner assy, a condenser assy and a working fluid reservoir. All installed to the chassis framework with 4 mounting fasteners each.

New propulsion system

An illustration of the four major assemblies bolted on a Ford chassis frame approximately as shown.

For planning and further discussions, a breakdown of key assembly components with part numbers and descriptions are presented in a list as follows:

ITEM	PART NO.	DESCRIPTION
1	D2351-100	Total propulsion system
2	D2351-200	Power plant assy
3	D2351-200-100	Reciprocating engine assy
4	D2351-200-100-10	Cylinder-piston assembly
5	D2351-200-100-10-1	Main cylinder-piston assy
6	D2351-200-100-10-2	Valve assy
7	D2351-200-100-10-3	Input chest assy
8	D2351-200-100-10-4	Exhaust chest assy
9	D2351-200-100-20	Internal assembly
10	D2351-200-100-20-1	Cross head assy
11	D2351-200-100-20-2	Stephenson Linkage assy
12	D2351-200-100-20-3	Crankshaft assy
13	D2351-200-100-20-4	Drive assy
14	D2351-200-100-20-5	Spline pad interface
15	D2351-200-100-30	Casing assy
16	D2351-200-200	External assy
18	D2351-200-300	Chassis mount frame assy
19	D2351-300	Boiler-burner assy
20	D2351-300-100	Boiler assy
21	D2351-300-200	Burner assy

New propulsion system

22	D2351-400	Condenser assy
23	D2351-500	Working fluid reservoir assy
24	D2351-600	Reverse lever assy
25	D2351-700	Electrical
26	D2351-800	Connection assy

Power-plant assembly

A two-cylinder cross-compound double-acting reciprocating engine includes external components linked to the driveshaft using standard 4L fan belts and pulleys. The alternator is shown mounted above the assembly. The water and steering pumps are shown beneath the assembly Engine input and exhaust ports are attached with standard 1/4 NPT pipe fittings.

Illustration 1: Power-plant assembly

A split case cover is principally used to contain the grease applied on bearings, slide rods, gears, and the Stephenson Linkage. The engine is a very simple design with few moving parts compared to the hundreds which make up an internal combustion engine.

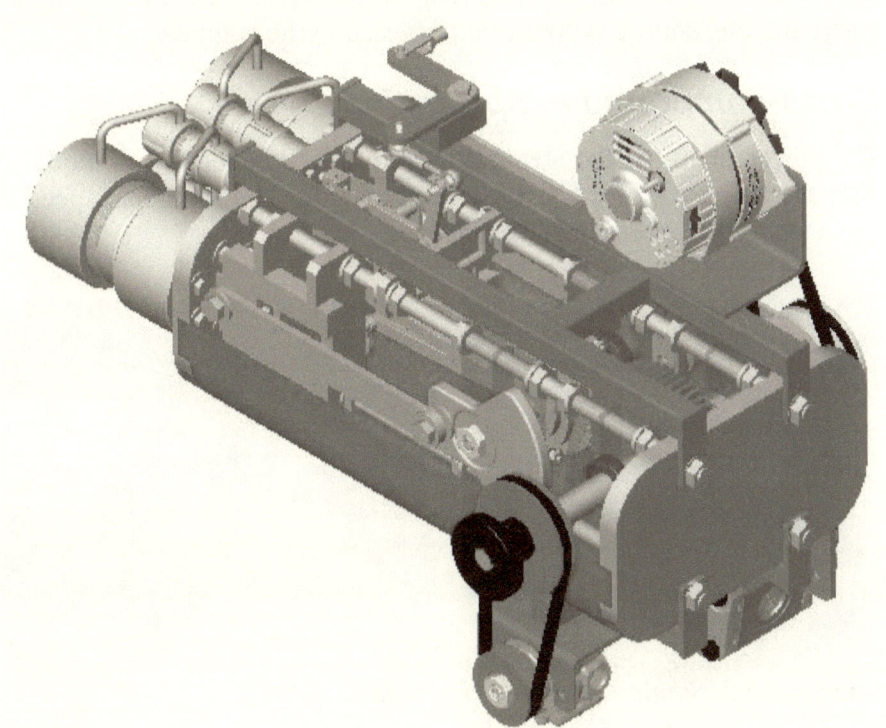

Illustration 2: Power-plant assembly shown with the chassis support structure removed

The engine is mounted to the rear-drive axle at a nominal 1.5 gear ratio between the engine's crankshaft and the differential gear.

Transmissions were not required and hence there is no "neutral" or clutch. Unlike the internal combustion-powered car where the engine provided the horsepower rating for the vehicle, a steam car was rated by its boiler's steaming capacity.

Thus horsepower ratings are capable of developing nearly 175 horsepower (290 hp) based on the analysis presented in a NASA TN D-5813 report.

Steam cars unitize an external combustion (Rankine cycle) engine where the fuel source is consumed external to the engine.

Cross-compound reciprocating engine

The power plant for the steam-powered design concept was modeled after the Stanley Motor Carriage steam engine. The rotational speed is expected to run approximately 600 rpm.

Illustration 3 Stanley Motor Carriage steam engine

The engine has two cylinders placed side by side. The steam is admitted to and exhausted from the cylinders with valves located between the cylinders known as slide valves. The valve gear arrangement is the Stephenson /Howe Linkage and is controlled from a lever bolted on the passenger floorboard.

New propulsion system

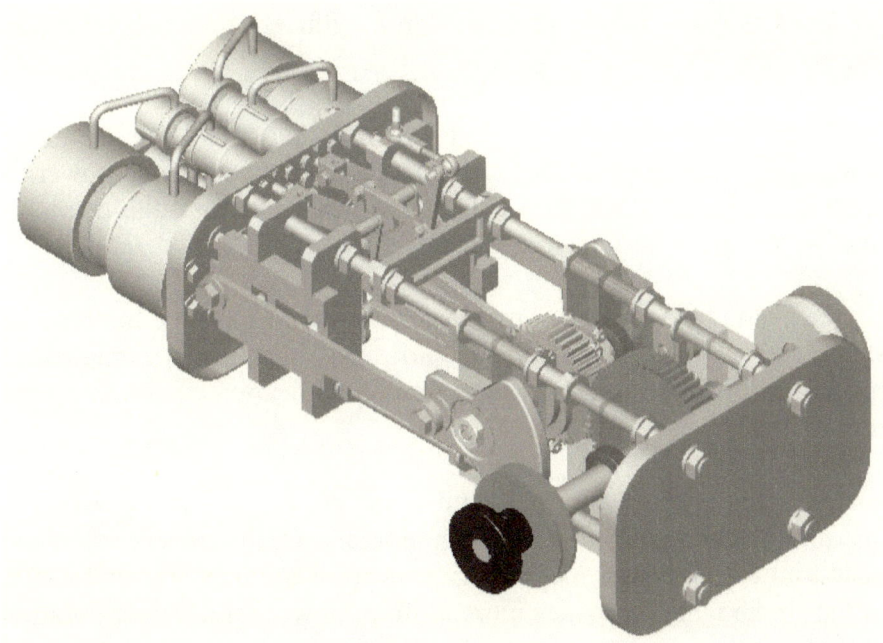

Illustration 4: Two-cylinder cross-compound double-acting reciprocating engine shown as an isometric solid model view

The engine is "double acting". This means that pressure is applied to both sides of the piston as the engine operates. The 3-inch piston is pushed by steam to one end of the cylinder (the cylinder is 4 inches long) and then it is pushed in the opposite direction by steam.

The internal combustion engine's pistons are only pushed in one direction from the explosion caused by igniting the air-fuel mixture. This means that the steam engine's pistons produce power every stroke they make in the engine's cylinder as compared to the internal combustion engine where the piston only produces power for 1 in 4 strokes it makes within the cylinder.

Thus in one revolution of the crankshaft, a two-cylinder steam engine produces as many power strokes as an 8 cylinder internal combustion engine does.

The engine provides four power impulses per crankshaft rotation similar to an 8-cylinder internal combustion engine. The power is applied uniformly for a longer length of the stroke than the hammer-like explosions common to gasoline or diesel engines.

By the piston being actuated by the cushion-like expansive force of the steam there is less pounding and jarring of mechanical components resulting in a highly uniform and steady application of power to the rear wheels.

Additionally, with the internal combustion engine, cylinder pressure is maximum at the moment of fuel ignition and rapidly tapers off as the piston moves. With the steam engine steam is admitted for up to 80% of the stroke which provides more uniform power for a longer duration of the stroke.

The long stroke of the steam cylinder along with a continuous even push of the piston much of the length of the cylinder provides the steam engine advantage of more torque in a smaller package over what can be generated with a gasoline engine of equivalent rating.

There's more power per pound in the steam engine than in an internal combustion engine of equivalent crank-horsepower.

Cylinder-piston assembly

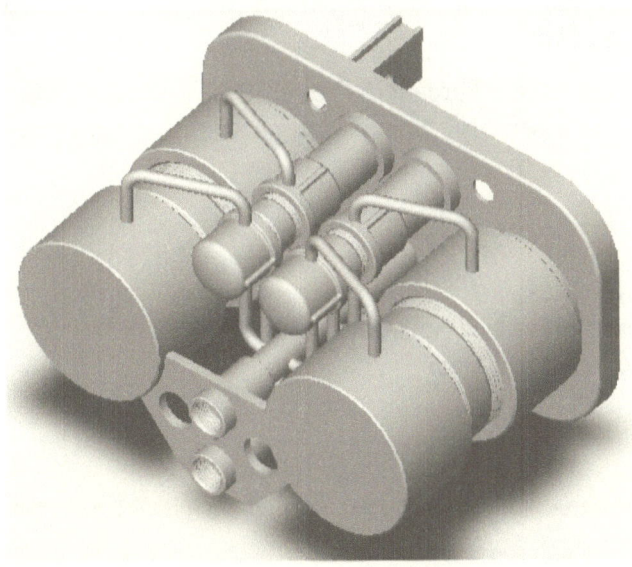

Illustration 5 Cylinder-piston assembly shown in an isometric view

The design concept cylinder-piston assembly includes two cylinders, two pistons, two sliding valve assemblies, one input and output steam chest with steam pipe connections. Some brazing is required to secure the feed and exhaust ports.

The two power cylinder-piston assemblies and two sliding valves assemblies are mounted on the front closure panel. The input and exhaust chest are also mounted on the panel with standard NPT type fittings.

A support plate attached to the main cylinder assemblies and the input and exhaust steam chest is brazed as shown in the illustration.

The cylinder housings for the valve and power piston cylinders are rated for 3000 psi pressure.

The cylinders are arranged side by side. The tubing configuration may be arranged in which the steam progressively expands in two or more cylinders.

New propulsion system

Main cylinder-piston assy

The double-acting cylinder-piston is one which steam is admitted alternately to each side of the piston.

High-Pressure Iron and Steel Threaded Pipe Fittings for use with steam are included in the assembly. Specifications are:

1. Class: 3000
2. Specifications Met: ANSI/ASME B16.11, ASTM A105, ANSI/ASME B1.20.1
3. Pipe Nipples and Pipe: Use Schedule 160 steel
4. Flanges: Use Class 1500 steel

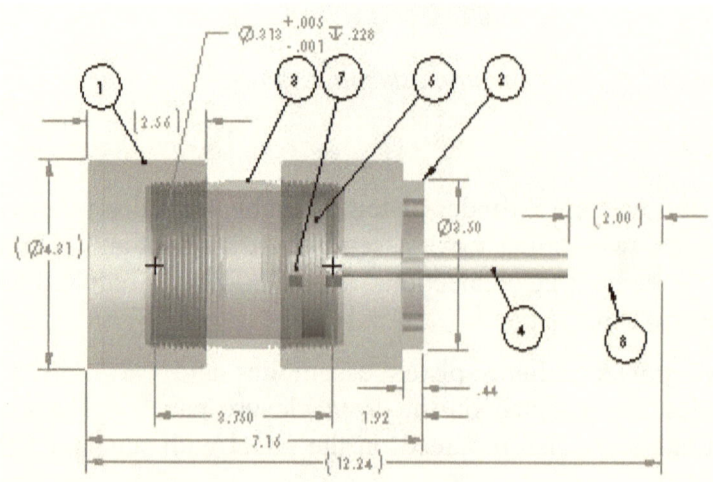

Illustration 6: **Main cylinder-piston assy**

Valve assembly

The slide valve is a valve which controls the inlet and exhaust of steam by sliding across the ports.

 The valves should be properly adjusted for the maximum amount of

New propulsion system

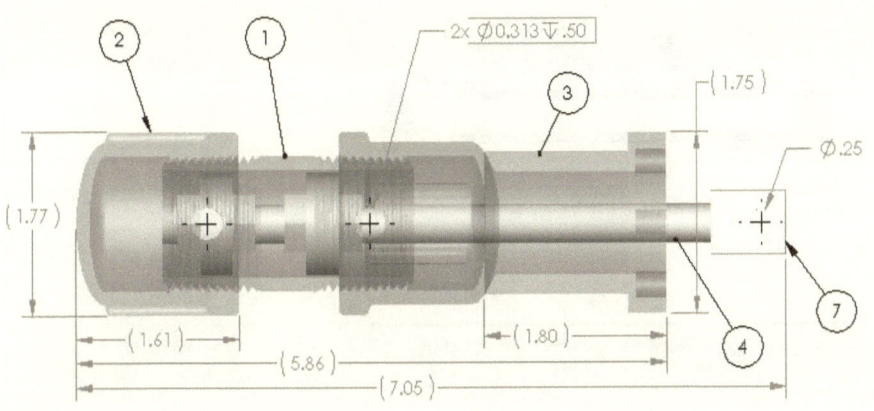

Illustration 7: Valve assembly

work output delivered per cycle. Fortunately, a method is available by turning item 7 in quarter-turn increments in the clockwise or counterclockwise direction. After the engine is assembled, it is connected and driven with shop air for final adjustments.

Input chest assy

The input chest assembly includes 3 standard pipe fittings. The 4512k62 fitting is threaded on each end of the 44615k474 fitting. The 44615k474 fitting is modified with 2 throught holes as shown in the illustration.

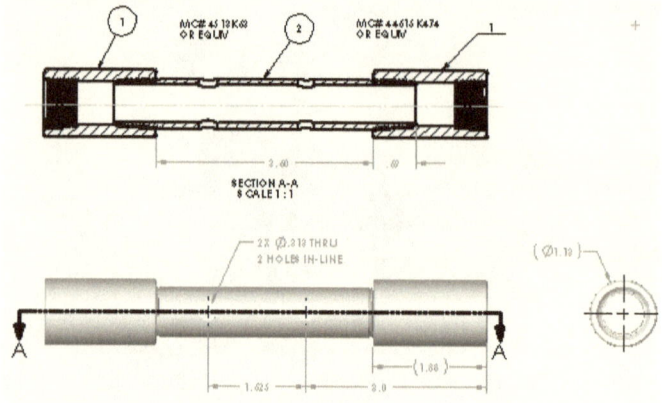

Illustration 8 Input chest assy

Exhaust chest assy

The input chest assembly includes 3 standard pipe fittings. The 4512k62 fitting is threaded on each end of the 44615k474 fitting. The 44615k474 fitting is modified with one through hole as shown in the illustration.

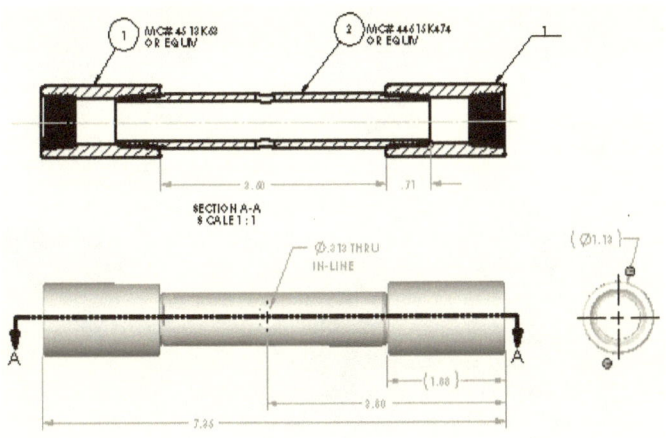

Illustration 9 Exhaust chest assy

Internal assembly

The Internal assembly includes six subassemblies listed as follows:

1. Crankshaft assembly
2. Stephenson Linkage assembly
3. Driveshaft assembly
4. Crosshead support assembly
5. Propeller adapter assembly
6. Rear panel assembly

The crosshead support assemblies include an opposite configuration for each cylinder. The same parts are used in both assemblies but different configurations.

Four standard threaded rods, 5/8-11 UNC-2A x 23 inches long are used to secure all the subassemblies in the proper orientation. The Internal assembly is easily attached to the Cylinder-piston assembly with fasteners provided.

New propulsion system

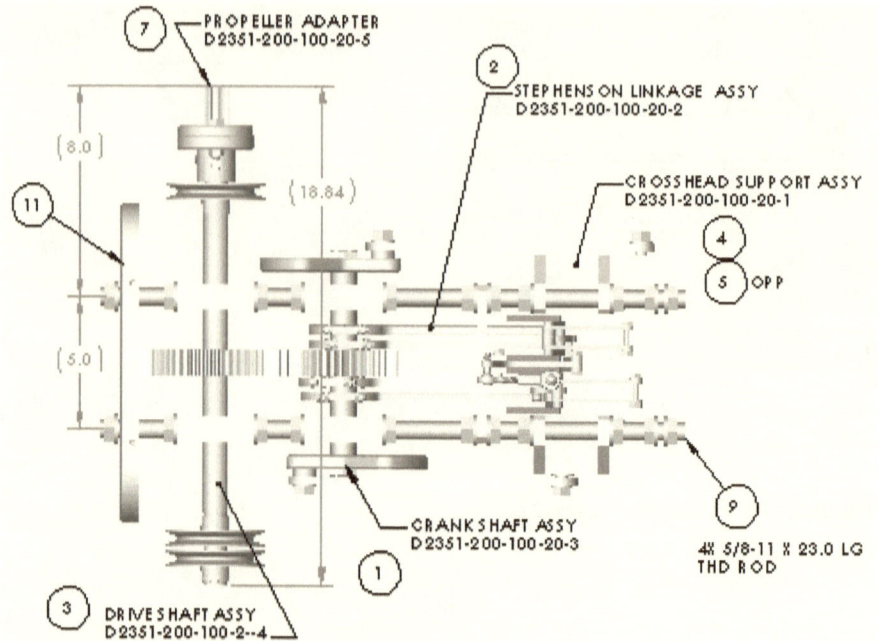

Illustration 10 **Internal assembly**

Crosshead support assy

The crosshead assembly includes an opposite assembly. The slide portion is made from Grade 142 Rulon which is bronze filled and often used to fabricate linear slides and piston rings

- − Temperature Range: -400° to 550° F
- − Tensile Strength: 2,000-3,100 psi
- − Impact Strength: 6 ft.-lbs./in. (Excellent)
- − Hardness: Not Rated (Medium)

Rulon PTFE, a PTFE material that's been modified with an epoxy-coated fiber. In addition to having the superior chemical and temperature resistance of PTFE, they have excellent impact resistance and a super-slippery surface that resists wear. These easy-to-machine sheets are nonabsorbent, so they won't swell when exposed to water.

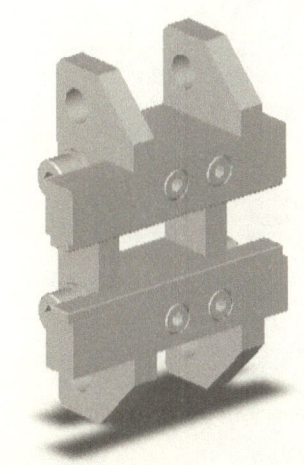

Illustration 11 Crosshead support assy -1 shown -2 opposite

Stephenson Linkage assy

During the 1830s the most popular valve drive for locomotives was known as *gab motion* in the U.K. and *V-hook motion* in the U.S.A.

In 1841 two employees in Stephenson's locomotive works, draftsman William Howe and pattern-maker William Williams, suggested the simple expedient of replacing the gabs with a vertical slotted link, pivoted at both ends to the tips of the eccentric rods. To change direction, the link and rod ends were raised or lowered employing a counterbalanced bell crank worked by a *reach rod* that connected it to the reversing lever.

New propulsion system

The linkage designed to set the timing and reverse function for the

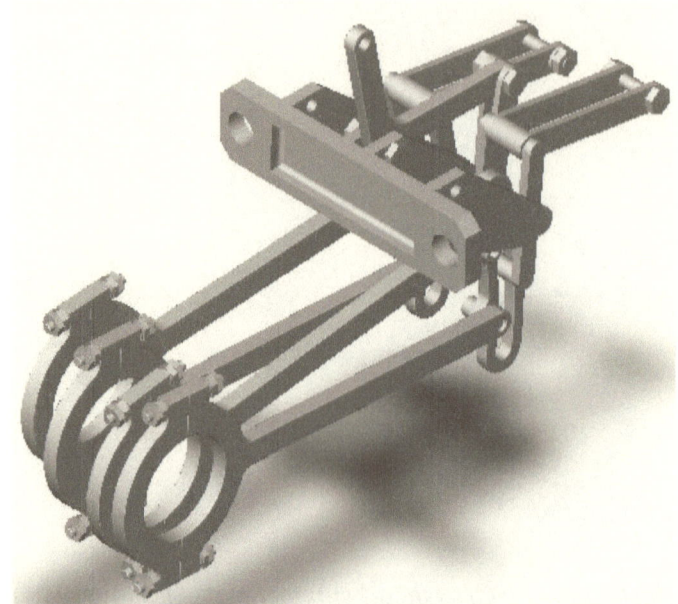

*Illustration 12: **Stephenson Linkage assy shown in an isometric view***

cross-compound reciprocating engine herein is shown in the solid model isometric view.

Crankshaft assy

The crankshaft assembly includes a 4.2 diameter spur gear, 4 cams (items 27,29,30 and 31), and 2 flywheel weights mounted on a 7/8 diameter keyway shaft. The power-transmission elements and cams are located close to the supporting bearings.

The gear manufacturer is RushGears.com. The part number is F1040 with a pitch type DP. Also, pitch is 10, PD is 4, number of teeth is 40, pressure angle is 20 degrees, the outside diameter is 4.2, the face is 1.0 inches, the bore is 0.875 diameter, keyway width is 0.1875, depth is 0.0938, service factor is 1.25 and the duty cycle is continous. The

New propulsion system

material is 440F SS.

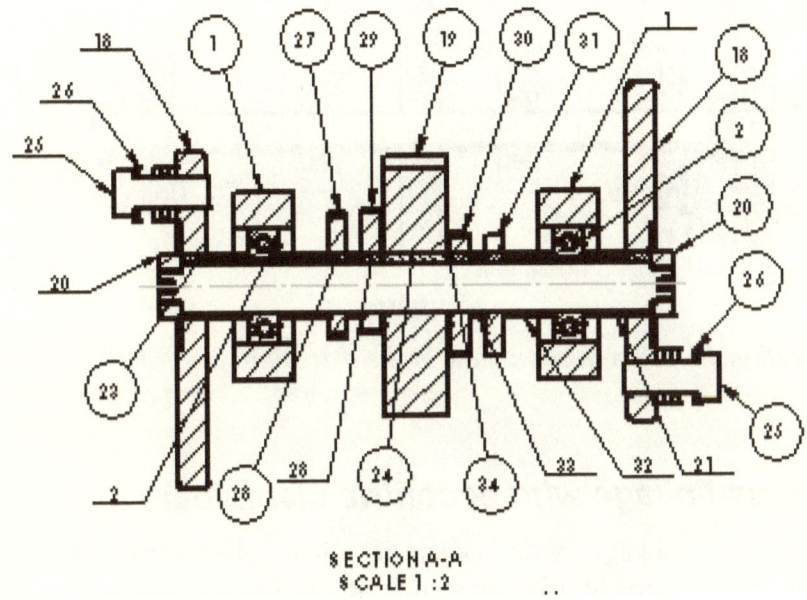

Illustration 13 Section view of the Crankshaft assembly

Driveshaft assy

The driveshaft assembly includes a 6.2 diameter spur gear, 3 pulleys, and hub adapters all mounted on a 7/8 diameter keyway shaft. The power-transmission element is located close to the supporting bearings.

The gear manufacturer is RushGears.com. The part number is F1060 with a pitch type DP. Also, pitch is 10, PD is 6, number of teeth is 60, pressure angle is 20 degrees, the outside diameter is 62, the face is 1.0

inches, the bore is 0.875 diameter, keyway width is 0.1875, depth is 0.0938, service factor is 1.25 and the duty cycle is continous. The material is 440F SS.

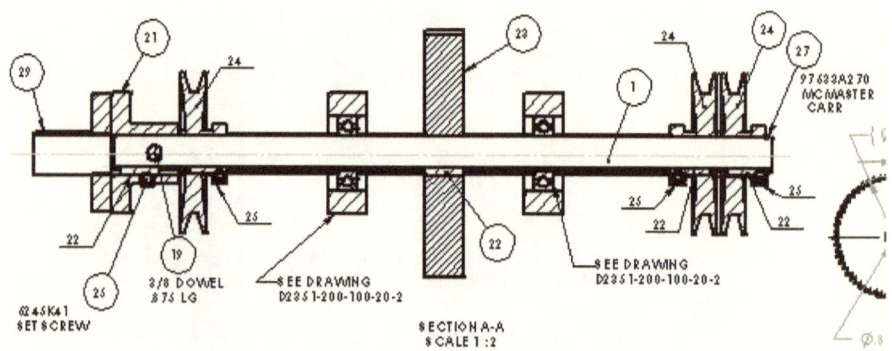

Illustration 14 Cross Section view of the driveshaft assembly

Reverse linkage with eccentric clamp bars

The reverse linkage with eccentric clamp bars was designed specifically to provide a linear switch action for the reverse function and valve timing sequence for proper steam input and cutoff.

Timing

The Stephenson style linkage was based on timing sequence requirements (steam cutoff) for both steam valve assembly and the power cylinder-piston assembly. A Stephenson link program was used in developing the critical timing linkage. Note, the Stephenson linkage is also used for forward and reverse changes.

Gears, bearings & cam-and-followers

The internal mechanism of the engine includes 2 gears, 2 bearings, and 4 cam-followers. The primary gear is a 40 tooth, 20-degree pressure angle gear. The mating secondary gear is a 60 tooth, 20-degree pressure angle gear in mesh at a 1:5 ratio. Radial roller bearings are

New propulsion system

used to support the gears and shaft loads.

Elastohydrodynamic lubrication (EHD) is the phenomenon that occurs when a lubricant is introduced between surfaces that are in pure rolling contact. The contact of gear teeth, rolling bearings, and cam-follower surfaces are typical examples. When a lubricant is trapped between two surfaces in rolling contact, a tremendous increase in the pressure within the lubricant film occurs. But viscosity is exponentially related to pressure and so a very large increase in viscosity occurs in the lubricant that is trapped between the surfaces.

The purposes of an antifriction-bearing lubricant may be summarized as follows:

1. To provide a film of lubricant between the sliding and rolling surfaces

2. To help distribute and dissipate heat-exchanger

3. To prevent corrosion of the bearing surfaces

4. To protect the parts from the entrance of foreign matter

Based on the following conditions, grease shall be used as the primary lubricant:

1. The temperature in the casing is not expected to go over 200 degrees F

2. The speed is low

3. Unusual protection is required from the entrance of foreign matter

4. Simple bearing enclosures are desired

5. The operation for long periods without attention is desired

Illustration 15 The internal mechanism of the engine includes gears, bearings and cam-followers. The primary gear is a 40 tooth, 20 degree pressure angle gear. The mating secondary gear is a 60 tooth, 20 degree pressure angle gear in mesh at a 1:5 ratio. Roller bearings are used to support the gears and power driven shaft loads. Cam – followers are used for the Stephenson linkages and crankshaft flywheels.

Testing and adjustments

After the engine is assembled, a standard shop air compressor may be used to test run the engine. Simply attach a standard air compressor fitting to the input port with 90-125 psi shop air pressure.

Final valve timing adjustments for steam cutoff is made by turning item 7 fitting on the valve piston a quarter turn clockwise or counterclockwise.

Power accessories

Provisions are made to include the alternator, steering and water pump with and external frame mounted on the two-cylinder cross-compound

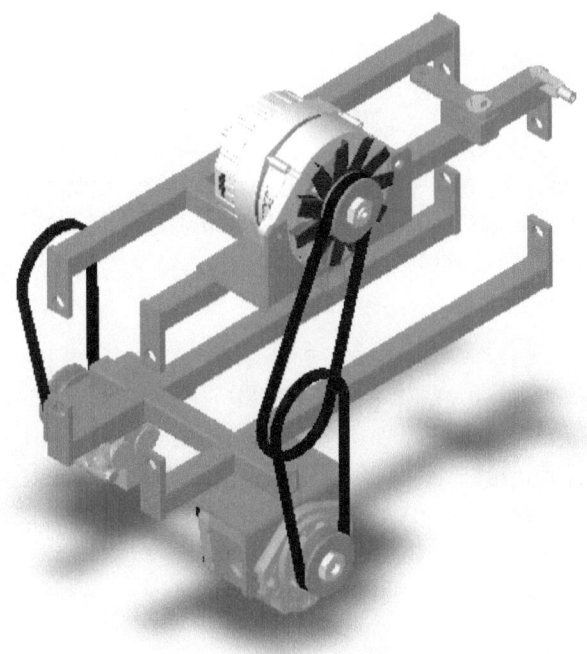

Illustration 16 Isometric solid model of the external assy. The power accessories are mounted on a frame. The frame is attached to the power-plant externally.

double-acting reciprocating engine.

The power accessories are mounted on a frame. The frame is attached to the power-plant externally.

Alternator

Alternators are used in modern automobiles to charge the battery and to power the electrical system when its engine is running. Automotive alternators require a voltage regulator which operates by modulating the small field current to produce a constant voltage at the battery terminals. A voltage regulator is normally mounted on the backside of the alternator housing.

Wiring harnesses for the alternator connections are included in all modern automobiles.

Steering Pump

The steering pump is used to provide hydraulic pressure to the automotive steering system. Power steering fills containers, input and return hoses, connection fittings included in all modern automobiles are used for the new propulsion system.

Water pump

The water pump is a key component in the Rankine cycle. It will provide the necessary water mass flow rates and pressure required for the system energy power output. A hydraulic pump from McMaster-Carr was selected in this case. Equivalent pumps may be used. The recommended mass flow rate per table II is 1484 lbs/hr.

Hydraulic pump

Hydraulic pump, also known as gear pumps, have few moving parts so they're less prone to wear than other hydraulic pumps. UN/UNF (SAE) thread connections have straight threads and are also known as O-ring Boss fittings. SAE A—4 3/16" Mounting Hole Center-to-Center

SAE A

Illustration 17 Hydraulic pump, also known as gear pumps, have few moving parts so they're less prone to wear than other hydraulic pumps.

Inlet Connection— UN/UNF (SAE)   1 5/16"-12-16

Outlet Connection— UN/UNF (SAE)   1 1/16"-12-12

7. Fixed Displacement Rate, cu. in./rev.   1.65

8. Max. Flow Rate, gpm   16.1

9. Max.Pressure, psi   2,700

10. Max. Speed, rpm   2,400Steam
    generator (Heat exchanger)

Steam Generator

The steam generator includes two principal components. The boiler and the burner. The mono-tube boiler-burner assembly is mounted on

Illustration 18   The steam generator includes two principle components. The boiler and the burner. The mono-tube boiler-burner assembly is mounted on a cross brace frame inside the engine compartment.

a cross-brace frame inside the engine compartment. A forklift or standard 20 pounds 4.7-gallon style propane tank is also installed inside the engine compartment and connected to a 200,000 BTU/hr burner.   For reference, in sizing the heat exchangers the calculations specified a 190,000 BTU burner. The water input is connected to the pump output on the reciprocating engine. Also, the water input is attached to the reservoir hot well output tube fitting to facilitate the initial start-up. The water exit tube fitting from the boiler is attached to the steam chest fitting locating in front of the engine. The throttle valve is attached to the accelerator pedal inside the passenger cab.

Boiler

Mono-tube boiler assembly

The mono-tube boiler assembly was designed based on the mathematical results as shown in table II. Forty rows of coils are laid in the boiler casing with a recommended transverse pitch of 1.0 and longitudinal pitch of 1.4 as specified in the boiler calculations.

Mono-tube coils

Fifty-foot lengths of welded 304 stainless steel coil tubing, 1/2" outside diameter, 0.460 inside diameter may be readily purchased off-the-shelf. The steel coil tubings may be welded or connected with swaged fittings to make up the total required length. The coils may be rolled by hand to make the recommended 1.0 transverse pitch. After fifty feed is hand-rolled then it is connected with proper fittings recommended for steam and continued with hand-rolling until all 40 rows with 6 coils per row are made.

The coils are then laid in the boiler casing with the recommended transverse and longitudinal dimensions.

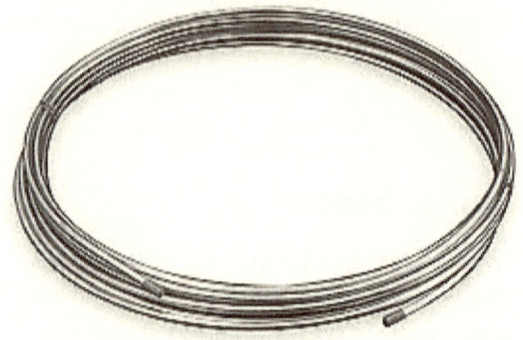

Illustration 19 Fifty feet sets of welded 304 stainless steel coil tubing, 1/2" outside diameter, 0.460 Inside diameter may be purchased off-the-shelf

A nut with two sleeves (ferrules) gives these fittings extra gripping power. The sleeves bite into the tubing as you tighten the nut, creating a strong seal. Also known as instrumentation fittings, they are made to tight tolerances for use in high-precision applications

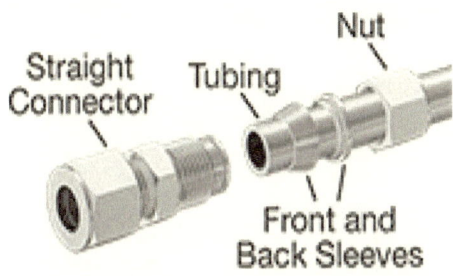

Illustration 20 A nut with two sleeves (ferrules) gives these fittings extra gripping power

Shell casing

The boiler shell casing and cap is made from steel sheet metal 16 gauge .06 inches thick. The sheet metal is wrapped around two16 gauge rings with mounting holes and brazed on each end of the shell casing. The seam of the sheet metal casing may also be brazed, or fastened with rivets or bolts. The dimensions are 1.1 feet in diameter and 1.68 feet high as reported in Table II.

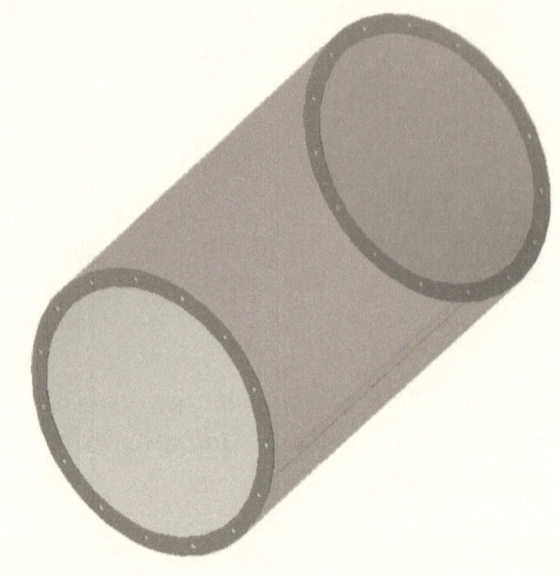

Illustration 21   The boiler shell casing and cap is made from steel sheet metal 16 gauge .06 inches thick. The sheet metal is wrapped around two rings with mounting holes and brazed on each end.. The seam of the sheet metal casing may also be brazed, or fastened with rivets or bolts.

Exhaust

The flue gas from the propane reaction is ejected thru the exhaust stack mounted in the steel boiler casing. A standard automobile tailpipe may be used as a flue gas exhaust component. The tailpipe placed through a hole cutout in the shell casing and brazed to the casing as shown.

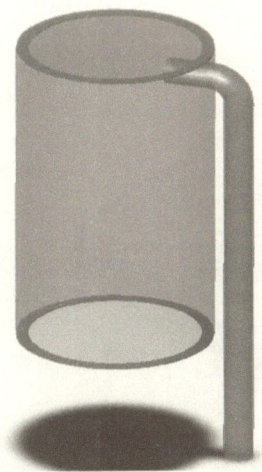

Illustration 22 The flue gas from the propane reaction is ejected thru the exhaust stack mounted in the steel boiler casing. A standard automoblie tail pipe may be used as a flue gas exhaust component. The tail pipe is brazed to the casing as shown.

Burner assembly

A 200,000 BTU/hr burner with propane hose connection and frame may be purchased from Amazon or eBay. A cover shell is attached to the burner frame.

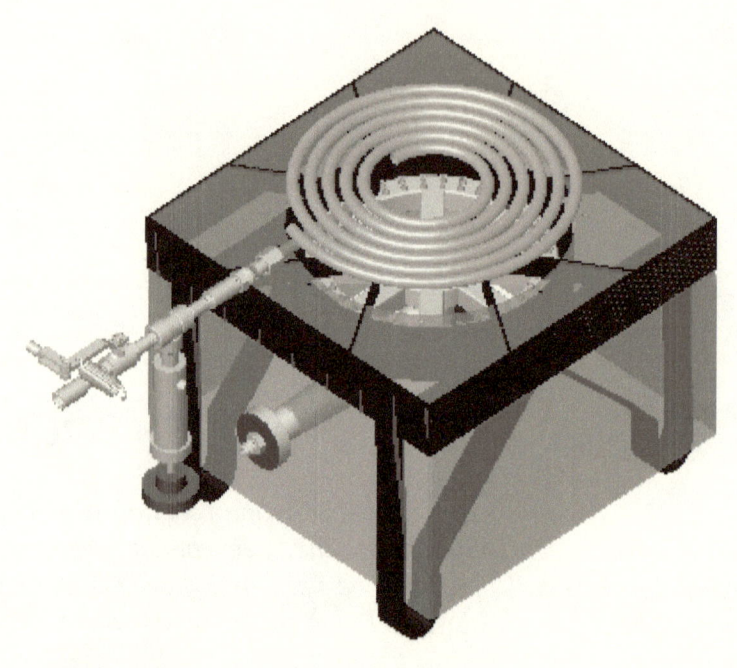

Illustration 23   A 200,000 BTU/hr burner with propane hose connection and frame may be purchased for Amazon or eBay. A cover shell is attached to the burner frame.

Illustration 24   A 200,000 BTU/hr burner with propane hose connection and frame

HIGH OUTPUT CAST IRON BURNER
Heavy duty high output cast iron burner
that is capable of 200,000 BTU

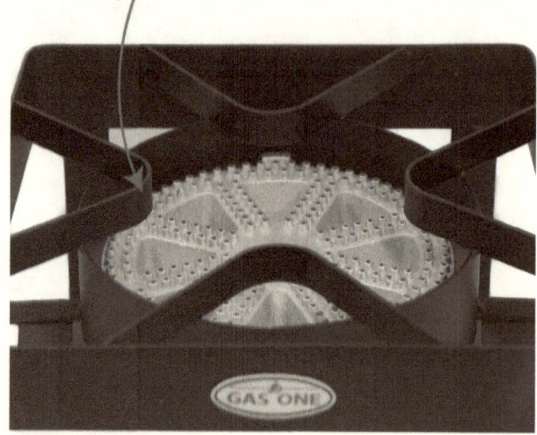

Illustration 25 A 200,000 BTU/hr burner with propane hose connection and frame

Spark IGNITOR

A Briggs & Stratton ignition coil magneto armature or equivalent may be included in the burner assembly for ignition. Spark plug not shown.

Auto Express Briggs & Stratton
Ignition Coil Magneto Armature
495859 491312 490586 492341
New
by Auto Express
★★★☆☆ ⌄   112 customer reviews
| 67 answered questions

Price: **$11.95** & **FREE Shipping**

Get $50 off instantly: Pay $0.00 $~~11.95~~ upon
approval for the Amazon Rewards Visa Card. No
annual fee.

Note: Available at a lower price from other sellers
that may not offer free Prime shipping.

- High Quality, New Design Ignition Coil
- Replaces Briggs & Stratton Part Numbers:
  492341, 491312, 490586, 495859
- Fits L-Head 10-13HP and Vanguard 9HP, 12.5HP,
  and 14HP

Compare with similar items

New (9) from $10.89 & FREE shipping.

Roll over image to zoom in

Illustration 26   spark ignitor

The spark ignitor should be used in conjunction with a rotating magnet flywheel as part of many standard lawnmower engines. An automotive windshield motor or equivalent may be used to turn the magnetic flywheel when the electronic sensor switch is turned on.

For automatic spark control and fuel management. A temperature-sensive resistor such as a thermistor may be incorpoated into a simple circuit to turn the spark ignitor and a 24 Vdc actuated Directional-Control Valves for Propane Gas (MC# 5184T123) installed between the propane hose connector, on and off automatically to conserve fuel based on temperature changes.

Illustration 27 A 24 Vdc actuated Directional-Control Valves for Propane Gas

Throttling valve assembly

Steam engine speed is governed in two ways: by throttling the steam supply, or by varying the cutoff.

The throttling valve assembly is used to control the steam engine speed in the new propulsion system.

The throttling valve assembly includes an extension spring mounted on the handle of the steam valve. Also installed in the handle is a cable mount fitting to be attached to the gas pedal cable assembly.

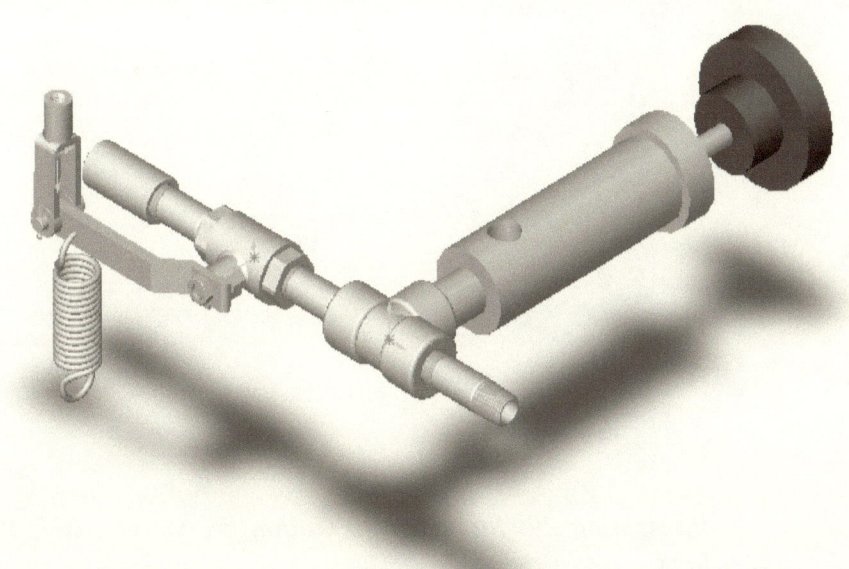

Illustration 28 The steam valve is shown with an extension spring and accelerator fitting attached to the lever. For reference a safety valve is shown to the right.

Fuel system

Standard propane tanks are used for the fuel source. 4.7-gallon tank is 12.2 inches diameter x 13.8 inches high. Forklift style tanks are the 7.9-gallon tank is 12.2 inches diameter x 21.8 inches tall.

New propulsion system

Illustration 29 Standard 20 Gallon propane tank

Combustion chemical energy

The boiler burner is an open-system steady flow combustion process. Fuel and oxidizer enter the system and combustion products leave the system. For reference, the energy equation for this process can be written as follows:

$$Q_{out} = \sqcup \, N_R \, (h_f^o + \Delta h)_R - \sqcup \, Np \, (h_f^o + \Delta h)_p$$

where: N is number of moles

h_f^o is enthapy of formation

h is enthapy of Products

The boiler burner runs on propane, C_3H_8, the balanced chemical reaction with 100 percent theoretical air

New propulsion system

$$C_3H_8 + 5(O_2 + 3.76N_2) \rightarrow 3CO_2 + 4H_2O + 18.8N_2$$

The propane and air prior to combustion are at 25 degrees Celsius (298Kelvin), and after combustion the products are at 1,400 Kelvin.

Determine the enthalpy of formation for propane, carbon dioxide and water vapor.

At 1,400 Kelvin, water is in the vapor phase, so the enthalpy of formation, h_f^o for vapor is used.

$C_3H_8 = -103,900$ kJ / kmol

$CO_2 = -393,500$ kJ / kmol

$H_2O = -241,800$ kJ / kmol

$N_2 = 0$ kJ /kmol

Enthapy of Products, h at 1,400 Kelvin

$C_3H_8 = $ *Not present*

$CO_2 = 55,900$ kJ / kmol

$H_2O = 43,500$ kJ / kmol

$N_2 = 34,940$ kJ /kmol

Insert the enthapy terms into the energy equation

Qout = (1 kmol C3H8)(-103,900 kJ / kmol)

-(3 kmol CO2)(-393,500 kJ / kmol)

-(4 kmol H2O)(-241,800 kJ / kmol)

— (18.8 kmol N2)(34,940 kJ / kmol)

Solve

$Q_{out} = 1,045,000$ kJ kmol C_3H_8

Divide Qout by the molar mass of propane (44 kilograms per kilomol)

New propulsion system

and by 1000 to get answer in megajoules per kg fuel

$$Q_{out} = 23.8 \text{ MJ / kg fuel}$$

Determine fuel consuption rate of the total propulsion system based on 190,000 BTU/hr requirement (Table II)

$$190,000 \text{ BTU/hr} = 201 \text{ MJ / hr}$$

$$\dot{m} = 201 \text{ } MJ/hr \div 23.8 \text{ } MJ/kg = 8.45 \text{ } kg/hr$$

Reference Propane Conversion Value Table

Propane Conversion Value Table

Pounds	Gallons	BTU @ 60 F	Therms	Vol ft^3	Dia (in)	Height (In)	Tare Wt (lbs)
4.23	1	91502	0.9	36.38			
1	0.24	21594	0.2	8.59			
5	1.2	109802	1.1	43.66	8	8.6	10
10	2.4	219605	2.2	87.31	8.9	13.8	15
20	4.6	420909	4.2	167.35	12.2	13.9	18
30	6.8	622214	6.2	247.38	12.2	19.6	25
33.5	7.9	723415	7.2	287.62	12.2	21.8	36
33.5	7.4	677115	6.8	269.21	12.3	22.4	24
40	9.2	841818	8.4	334.7	12.2	25.6	32
43.5	9.9	905870	9.1	360.16	12.2	27.8	44
43.5	9.9	905870	9.1	360.16	12.3	28.8	25
50	11.4	1043123	10.4	414.73	15.1	21.8	42
60	13.7	1253396	12.5	498.41	12.2	37.4	46
100	22.9	2095396	21	833.1	15.1	41	70
200	45.6	4172492	41.7	1658.93	24	34.1	152
420	95.9	8775042	87.8	3488.84	30	45.6	278

Note: At the time of this writing, the current propane cost per gallon was $3.92

Safety valve

In round numbers, there is a stick of dynamite in a gallon of water.

New propulsion system

How close do you want to get? Steam, when superheated, is an invisible, super-radiant gas. It can burn to the bone. You can walk into a cloud of invisible superheated steam, take one breath and destroy your lungs. It takes about 3 minutes to die and there is nothing you can do about it.

A safety valve is included in the boiler – burner assembly. The safety

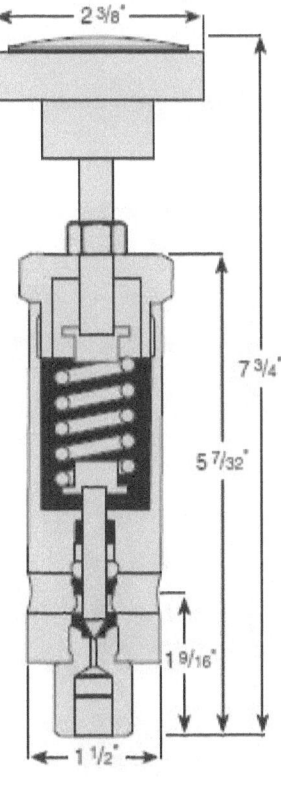

HIP-10-RV

Illustration 30   HIP-10-RV safety valve rated at 3000 psi pressure

valve selected for the concept system is rated at 3000 psi HIP-10_RV.

Condenser (Heat-exchanger)

Radiators are heat exchangers used to transfer thermal energy from one medium to another for cooling. This concept requires condensation of steam. Thermal energy is usually removed from a system by a condenser. **Every heat engine must reject heat – there's no way around it.** And it takes the same amount of energy you use to drive the engine to reject that heat.

Table I shows the detail results of sizing a condenser system in this case.

A typical radiator includes a 2 x 3-foot frontal area x 1.0 inch thick. The frontal area is acceptable, but the recommended thickness should be greater than 1 inch.

Illustration 31 Standard automobily radiator

The results recommend a radiator 6.0 inches thick. An alternative method is to place several standard radiators in tandem. Also, a fan shroud with 17 hp fans is recommended as shown in table I.

Illustration 32   Isometric view showing two standard radiators mounted in series on the chassis frame in the engine compartment. The radiators are supported on each end with angle brackets mounted on the frame. Straps are used to secure the radiators on the angles.

Working fluid reservoir

After the steam is condensed, it is dumped in a Working fluid reservoir

New propulsion system

(Also known as a hot well). The hot well may be purchased from McMaster-Carr or an equivalent water tank. The hot well may be mounted in the engine compartment or under the chassis frame structural support.

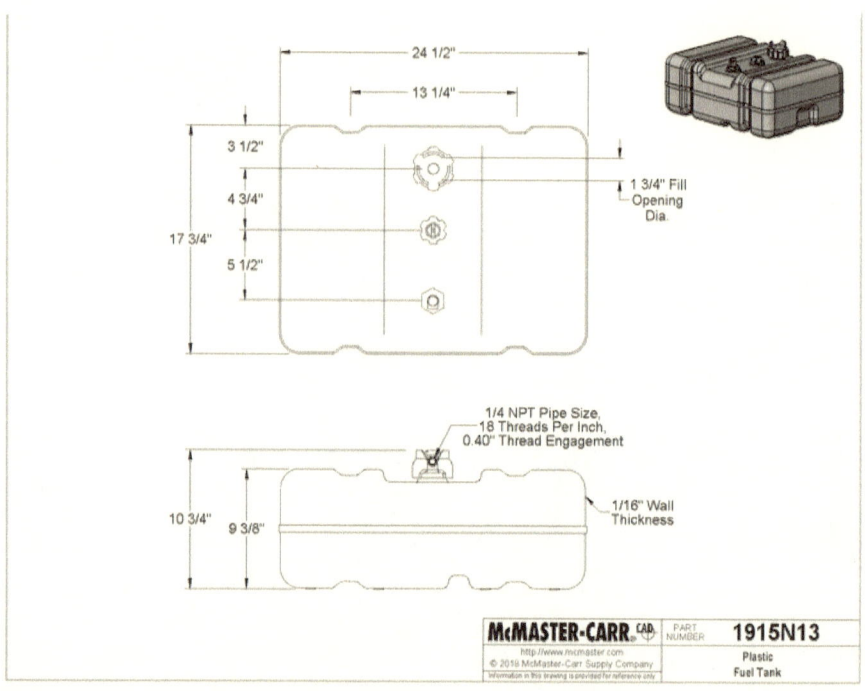

Illustration 33 The working fluid (hot well) tank may be purchased complete. The hotwell is mounted on two support beams mounted on the chassis frame.   Two steel bands are used to secure the HOTWELLl onto the beams.

Steam-oil Lubrication

The external parts of the steam engine should be greased periodically. As previously noted grease is applied to the pivot bolt on the crossheads, axles, gear teeth and crank bearings. However, the cylinder-piston may be lubricated by injecting a small amount of oil into the steam line.

Note, lubrication at high pressure and temperatures will find its way into the steam system where it breaks down. The hydrogen grabs the available oxygen first, leaving the carbon as deposits in the steam generator tubing. This was concerned until it was found that the Dobles running at 1200 F and 2000 psig appeared to show no major service problems in the early 1950s based on actual dynamometer test engine results.

The simplest type of lubrication system is a HYDROSTATIC lubricator. This system is mounted at any suitable vertical piece of the steam intake pipe. The principle behind the hydrostatic lubricator is that when 2 intake points in the steam line are balanced, the difference in pressure that injects the oil into the steam line is produced by the weight of water below the oil surface, stored in a small vessel.

Steam enters the upper pipe. The increased surface area of the condenser causes the steam to condense into water. The water drips down through the water valve and displaces the oil in the vessel. Since the oil floats on top and does not mix with water, it displaces out of the oil feed pipe. The regulating valve controls the amount of oil entering the steam line. The small check valve should be opened slowly from time to time to determine if there is still oil present in the container. After a while, you should be able to determine the average operating period that is possible in your engine case on one oil filling. The oil can be placed in the container through the oil fill plug. After draining the container through the drain plug and removing the condensed water. This, of course, should be done before the engine is started. Normally, any 2-cycle gas engine motor oil will work fine. To produce sufficient pressure to force the oil into the line, the length of the head pipe should be at least 18 inches. This simple hydrostatic lubricator can be easily built from simple copper plumbing with no problems.

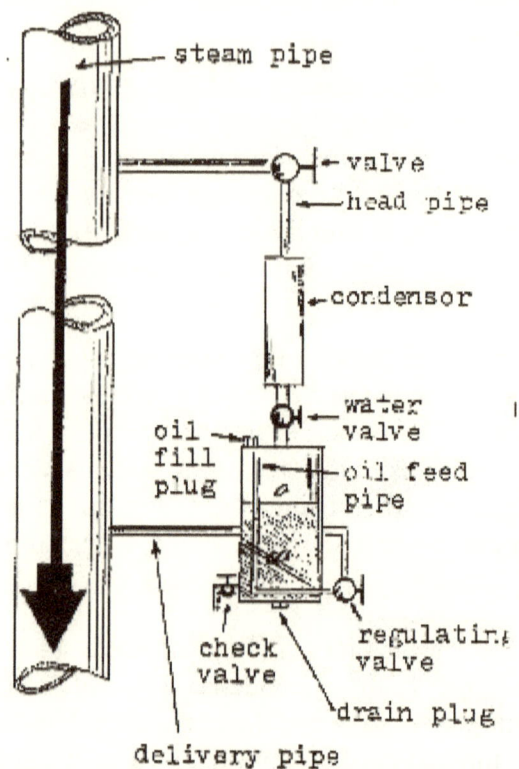

Illustration 34The simplest type of lubrication system is a HYDROSTATIC lubricator. This system is mounted at any suitable verical piece of steam intake pipe.

Platform

The design concept propulsion system may be installed in an existing vehicle platform with a rear differential gearbox and propeller shaft. In an example, an F150 Ford model pick up from a junkyard is used to convert the IC system into an EC system.

Illustration 35 Remove the IC engine, transmission, catalytic converter, mufflers, gas tank to make room for the new EC propulsion system

The internal combustion engine, transmission, muffler, catalytic converter, and gas tank are removed

Brake system

Most modern passenger vehicles use a vacuum assisted brake system that greatly increases the force applied to the vehicle's brakes by its operator. This additional force is supplied by the manifold vacuum generated by airflow being obstructed by the throttle on a running internal combustion engine. Since the IC engine shall be replaced, then an electrically operated vacuum pump should be installed to provide the necessary vacuum for the brake boost server.

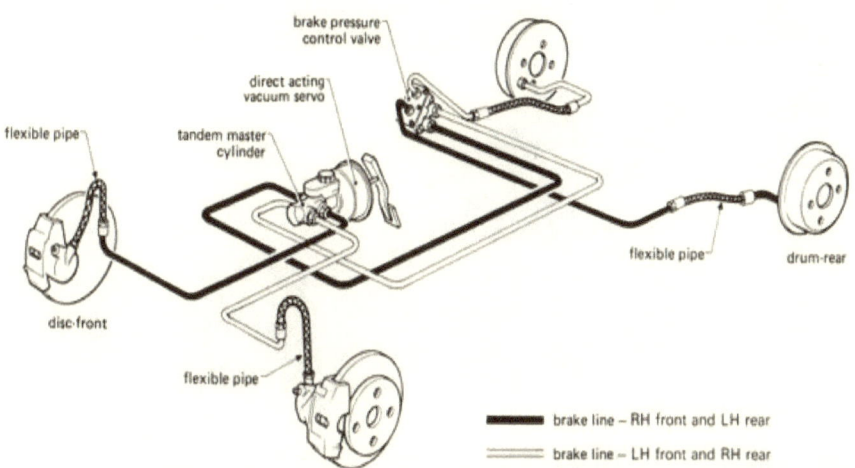

Illustration 36 A typical automoble braking system is shown. The key components are the direct acting vacuum servo, pressure control valve and the tandem master cyclinder.

Rear differential

In automobiles and other wheeled vehicles, the differential allows the outer drive wheel to rotate faster than the inner drive wheel during a turn. This is necessary when the vehicle turns, making the wheel that is traveling around the outside of the turning curve roll farther and faster than the other. The average of the rotational speed of the two driving wheels equals the input rotational speed of the drive shaft. An increase in the speed of one wheel is balanced by a decrease in the speed of the other.

*Illustration 37 The rear wheel fifferential gear model used in
the new propolsion system model is based on the ford rear end.*

When used in this way, a differential couples the longitudinal input
propeller shaft to the pinion, which in turn drives the transverse ring
gear of the differential.

Propeller shaft

A propeller shaft (prop shaft), or Cardan shaft is a mechanical
component for transmitting torque and rotation, usually used to
connect other components of a drive train that cannot be connected
directly because of distance or the need to allow for relative movement
between them. The adapter should be installed between the engine
drive flange and propeller shaft.

In this case, an adapter with a spline is used for the connection.

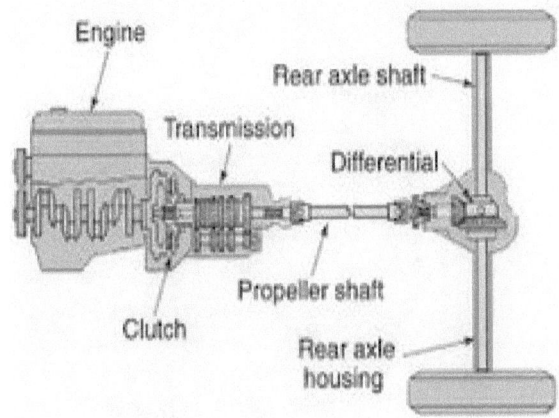

Illustration 38 After the engine and transmission is removed, the propeller shaft is attached to the new propulsion system power-plant.

Steering pump and reservoir

The steering pump pressure outlet on the engine must be connected to the power steering in the vehicle. The exit hose is connected to the steering pump reservoir.

The steering pump is relocated onto the external frame as previously mentioned. Line connections must be extended as required.

Illustration 39   The steering pump is mounted   externally   to   the   new propulsion   system   external   assy frame.

Electrical system

Since it is not possible to include all wiring diagrams for every vehicle, typical and most common electrical general information is used. Power for the lights and all electrical accessories is supplied by a lead/acid type battery that is charged by the alternator now located on the engine.

The battery is normally connected to a fusible link block and the solenoid starter. The fusible link block also is connected to the ignition switch in the steering column and the alternator.

Since the wiring harnesses are all connected properly. There should be no changes required for the alternator wiring diagram. The alternator should be connected to existing fuze links within the host vehicle and properly grounded.

Gas pedal and cable

The throttle, which controls fuel supply to the engine and is also known as the "accelerator" or "gas pedal", is normally the right-most floor pedal. It has a fail-safe design – a spring, which returns it to the idle position when not depressed by the driver.

Installation

The two-cylinder cross-compound double-acting reciprocating engine, boiler assembly and working fluid reservoir are attached to the chassis frame as shown.

Illustration 40: The two-cylinder cross-compound double-acting reciprocating engine, boiler assembly and working fluid reservoir are attached to the Ford chassis frame as shown. A Chevy Silverado extended cab pickup body with longer wheel base is shown for reference in scale only.

Power plant

The two-cylinder cross-compound double-acting reciprocating engine is installed on the chassis frame with four fasteners. A handheld drill motor is used to drill a 1/2 inch clearance hole through the chassis frame. Attach the propeller shaft spline connection onto two-cylinder cross-compound double-acting reciprocating engine adapter. Connect the steam input to the input chest assy located in front of the engine. Connect the steam output exhaust to the exhaust chest assy also located in front of the engine. Attach the Stephenson link reach rod to the lever assembly mounted on the floorboard inside the passenger cab.

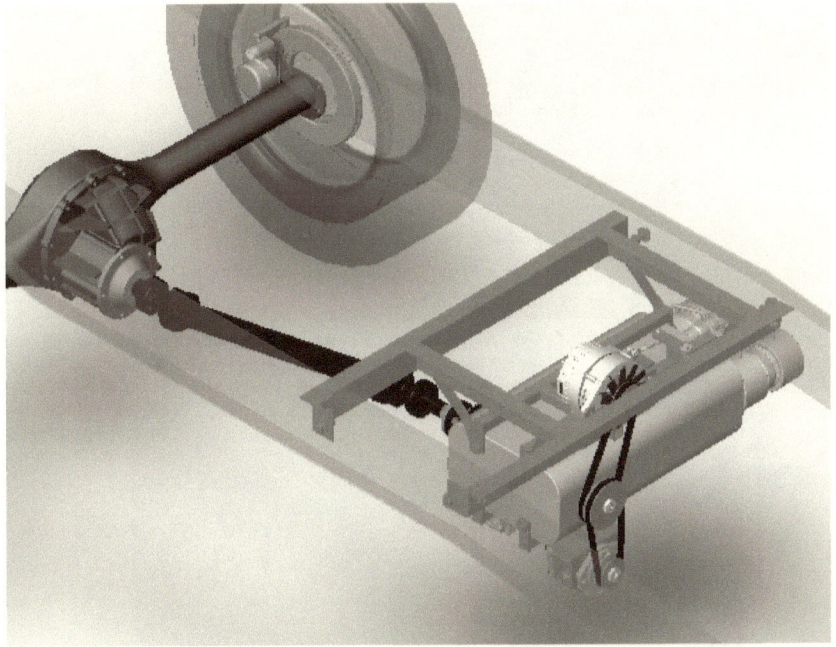

Illustration 41

Mono-tube boiler assembly

The mono-tube boiler-burner assembly is mounted onto the chassis inside the engine compartment. Two standard 4x3x1/2 ASTM A36 structural angles may be installed between the chassis with 1/2-13 UNC-2A fasteners. The mono-tube boiler-burner assembly calculated weight is 159 lbs. The z-section modulus is 1.85 $in^{3.}$ Maximum

New propulsion system

Stress in bending based on 3 foot lengths is 159 lbs x 1.5 ft x 12 in /ft / 1.85 in³ is 1547 psi. Should be more than adequate strength wise with an A36 yield strength of 36 Kips. The mono-tube boiler-burner assembly is secured on the legs of the angles with 1/2-13 UNC-2A fasteners.

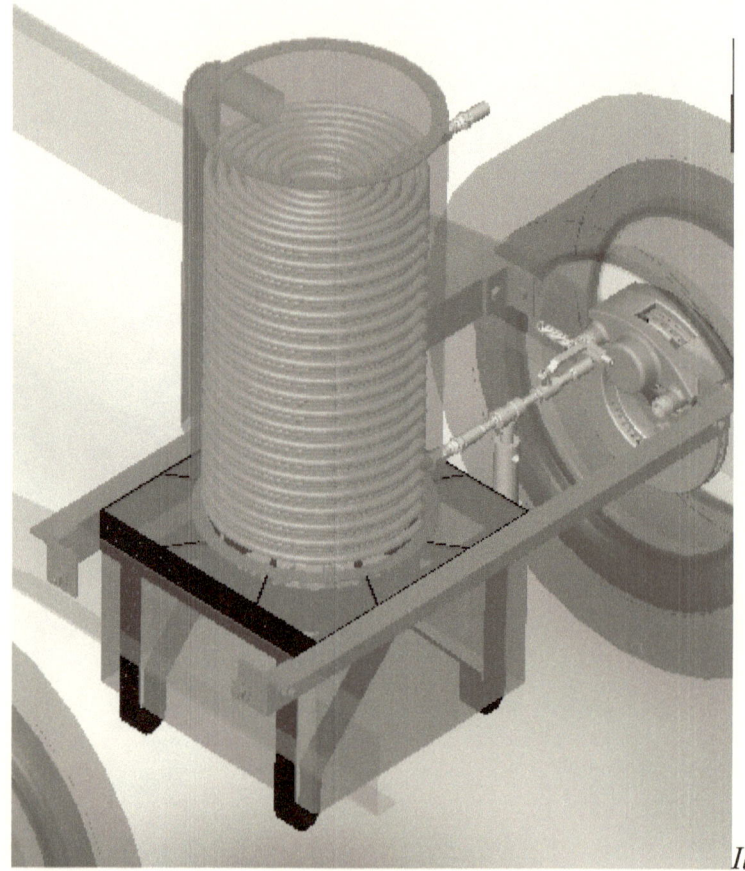

*Illustr
ation 42*

Attach the throttling cable on the throttle valve and the petal assembly inside the passenger cab. A forklift style or standard 20 pounds 4.7-gallon propane tank is installed inside and hooked up to the 200,000 BTU/hr burner. The water input from the pump on the reciprocating engine is installed to the boiler water input fitting. Also, the pump water input is attached to the hot well output tube fitting. The water exit tube fitting from the boiler is attached to the steam chest fitting. The throttle valve is attached to the accelerator pedal inside the cab.

Condenser assembly

If a standard radiator is not included in the acquired platform, then attach the condenser assembly (radiators) in the engine compartment. Attach the hose input of the condenser to the steam output exhaust in the steam piston/cylinder powered engine assembly. Attach the hot well exit fitting to the pump input fitting. Attach the pump output fitting to the mono-tube boiler input fitting.

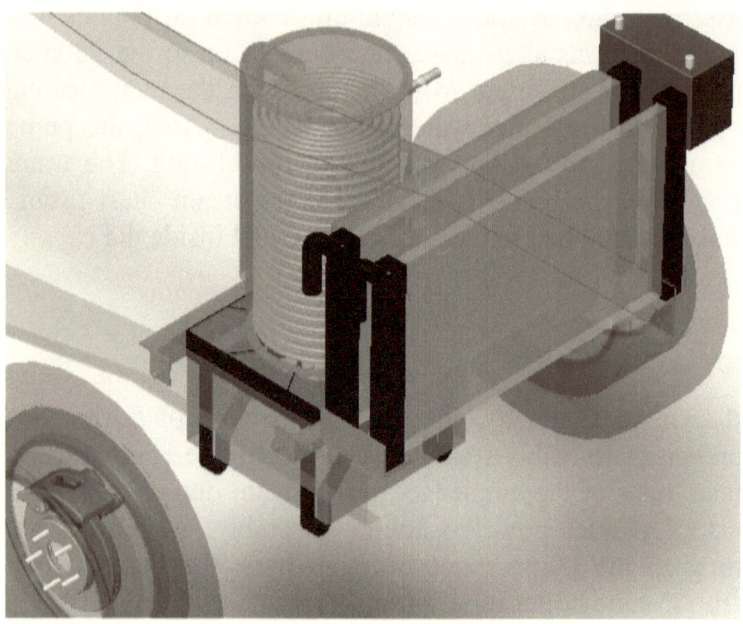

Illustration 43

Working fluid reservoir

The Working fluid reservoir hot well is mounted between the chassis frame in the engine compartment.

Again, attach two standard 4x3x1/2 ASTM A36 structural angles between the chassis for support with 1/2-13 UNC-2A fasteners. The Working fluid reservoir hot well capacity is 12 gals. One gallon of water equal to 8.4 lbs. Total weight is 12 x 8.4 = 101 lbs . The z-section modulus is 1.85 in³· Maximum Stress in bending based on 3 foot lengths is 101 lbs x 1.5 ft x 12 in /ft / 1.85 in³ is 982 psi. Should be adequate for strong support.

New propulsion system

Illustr
ation 44

Nylon or steel straps may be used to secure the hotwell reservoir in place.   Steel shipping straps crimped may also be used.

Inline automotive solenoid fuel pump

To get the system started we need to pressurize the water. A compression process using a work input is required to increase the water pressure. In early times, hand pumps were used and may still be used for the initial start-up. However, since a 12 volt DC automotive-style electrical system will be part of the system, we shall install an inline solenoid pump component to provide the initial work for pressurizing the system. A Spectra Premium Gasoline/Diesel Fuel Pump A8016EP is shown for example.

The inline automotive solenoid fuel pump is installed to extract liquid

New propulsion system

water from the water (hot well) reservoir to the input connection in the mono-tube boiler.   A check valve is used to insolate the solenoid pump from the water pump. The electrical power is provided by the 12 Vdc battery with a momentary switch to start the engine.

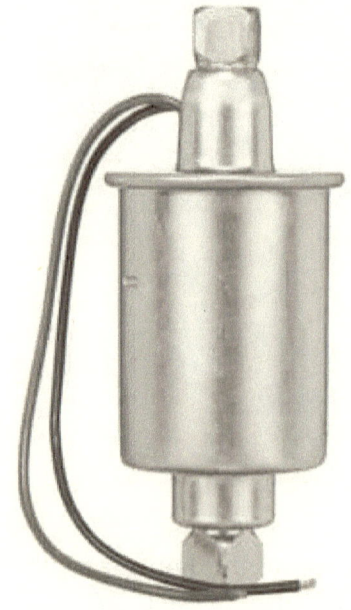

Illustration 45   Spectra Premium Gasoline/Diesel Fuel Pump A8016EP or equivalent

Product Details

Part Number:	A8016EP
Weight:	1.02lbs
Warranty:	Limited Lifetime
Application:	Electric Fuel Pump 25 GPH
Gaskets Included:	No
Inlet Attachement:	Threaded
Inlet Count:	1

New propulsion system

Inlet Size:	1/8-27
Item Grade:	OEM Standard
Maximum Free Flow Rate (gph):	34.0
Maximum Pressure Range (psi):	5.0
Minimum Free Flow Rate (gph):	21.0
Minimum Pressure Range (psi):	2.5
Outlet Attachment:	Threaded
Outlet Count:	1
Outlet Size:	1/8-27
Package Contents:	Pump & Kit
Product Condition:	New
Pump Location:	External
Strainer Included:	Yes
Wiring Harness Included:	No

A little steam-powered theory

The steam-powered system follows a process known as the Rankine cycle. In any thermodynamic cycle, the fluid goes through several different processes and returns to its initial state at the end of a cycle. The Rankine cycle uses water as the working fluid to generate power with an engine.

When most people hear about steam engines they think of old train engines that huff and puff a disappearing trail of steam while belching out clouds of black smoke. This kind of engine uses high-pressure steam that does work by expanding the steam against a piston in a cylinder. Steam engines may seem old fashioned, but they are still used every day in a different form to generate power.

In the modern steam engine water goes through four thermodynamic processes to complete an ideal cycle:

1. A compression process using a work input increases the water pressure.
2. A heat input process generates steam from liquid water.
3. An expansion process in a piston or turbine gets work out of the engine.
4. A condensation process gets heat out of the system and turns the steam to its liquid state.

The figure shows a diagram of the four components in the Rankine cycle.

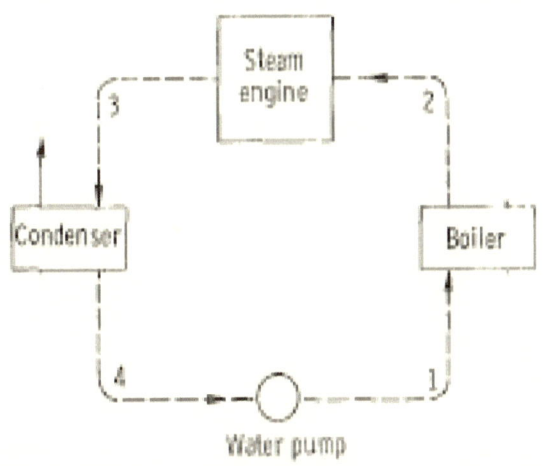

Illustration 46 diagram of the four components in the Rankine cycle

Here's how the components contribute to the thermodynamic cycle:

Pump: The pump pressurizes the water between states 4 and 1 as shown in the figure and sends it through the boiler to turn it into steam.

Steam generator: The steam generator (or boiler) consists of a firebox where fuel burns. You see it between states 1 and 2 in the figure. The walls of the firebox are lined with tubes filled with high-pressure water. As the water boils in the tubes, it turns into steam and flows into a heat exchanger located in the hottest part of the boiler. The steam becomes superheated.

Steam engine: The steam engine is a reciprocating piston/cylinder device that is used to extract work from the steam as shown between states 2 and 3 in the figure.
Condenser: After the steam goes through the engine in the Rankine cycle, it's condensed back into the water. The steam condensation process takes place in a heat exchanger that circulates air (or water) over a series of steam filled tubes. This heat exchanger is called a condenser.

The Rankine cycle

To understand how the Rankine Cycle works is to see the thermodynamic path taken by each of the four processes. A temperature-entropy (T-s) diagram is shown in the figure :

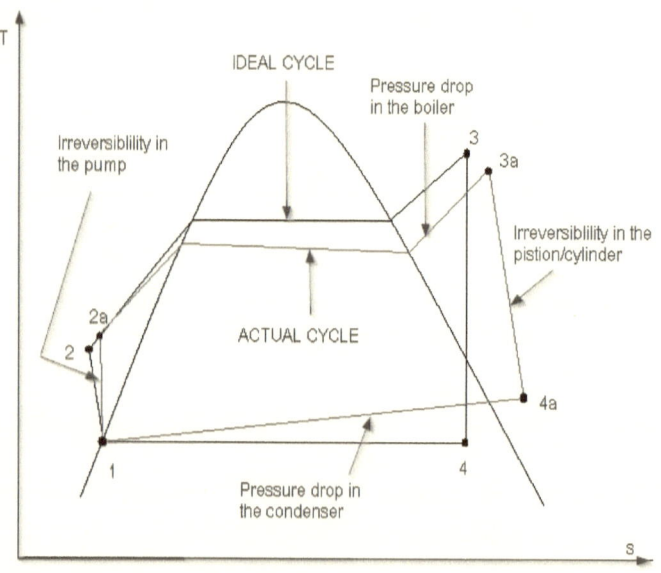

Illustration 47   temperature-entropy (T-s) diagram

Where the inverted u-shaped line is called the liquid-vapor dome. It represents the liquid to vapor transition region in the phase diagram. The portion of the line on the left side of the peak is 100 percent liquid, and the portion on the right side of the peak is 100 percent vapor. The area beneath the liquid-vapor line is a mixture of liquid and vapor. The area to the left of the liquid line is called the compressed liquid, while the area to the right of the vapor line is called superheated vapor.

The four processes of the Rankine cycle are as follows:

Work in, isentropic compression

Water is pressurized by isentropic compression in a pump to the operating pressure of the steam generator The line from State 1 to State 2 on the T-s diagram shows this process. The compression process in the ideal pump is reversible (frictionless) and adiabatic (transfer no heat from the pump). Because it's reversible and adiabatic, the process is isentropic, meaning that entropy is constant.

Heat in at constant pressure

The steam generator (or boiler) adds heat to the water to produce high-temperature steam. The line from State 2 to State 3 on the T-s diagram shows this process.

The water temperature increases from State 2 as heat is added until it reaches the boiling point. Then the temperature remains constant until the water becomes a vapor.

Finally, additional heat causes the vapor temperature to continue rising to State 3. Because water boils into a vapor only if the operating pressure is less than the critical pressure of 22 megapascals, this steam generator is called a subcritical steam generator. Boiling doesn't take place above the critical pressure, and the fluid simply increases in temperature without a phase change, meaning the steam generator is a supercritical steam generator. In the ideal steam generator, pressure remains constant, and the process is therefore isobaric.

Work out, isentropic expansion

The high-temperature and high-pressure steam have a lot of energy when it leaves the steam generator. Work is extracted from the steam by isentropic expansion in an engine. The vertical line from State 3 to State 4 on the T-s diagram shows this process.

New propulsion system

As steam flows through the engine, the pressure, and temperature decrease so the specific volume of the steam increases. The steam can become a liquid-vapor mixture in the final stages of the engine.

In practice, the minimum quality of the liquid-vapor mixture leaving the engine is 90 percent. The quality of the steam is a measure of moister content(liquid water) in the steam. This means the steam mixture must contain less than 10 percent liquid water by mass; otherwise, water droplets impacting the engine blades at high speed can cause pitting and erosion on the blades. The lower case x usually represents the thermodynamic property of steam quality.

Heat out at constant pressure

As the steam leaves the engine, it condenses back into liquid water in a constant pressure process from State 4 to State1, as shown in the T-s diagram. The water is condensed into a liquid because pressurizing a liquid takes a lot less work than pressurizing a gas.

At the exit of the condenser, the water is often a saturated liquid, which means it has a liquid-vapor quality of 0.0.

Analyzing the Rankine cycle

In the thermodynamic analysis of any Rankine cycle, you need to find thermodynamic properties at each state. Steam tables are useful in reducing the required mathematical equations.

In the following example, you can find the pump work, heat engine work, heat input, heat rejected, and steam quality at the exit. Imagine a cycle with heat engine inlet conditions (State 3) at 10 megapascals, 800 degrees Celsius. The condenser pressure (at State 1 or State 4) is 10 kilopascals. The steam mass flow rate through the system is 60 kilograms per second.

You can analyze this simple Rankine cycle by the following steps:

Pump inlet

Determine the thermodynamic properties at State 1, the pump inlet.

At State 1, the pressure is 10 kilopascals, and the water is a saturated liquid. This means the quality (x_1) is 0.0. Use these two independent thermodynamic properties to find the following properties from steam tables by interpolation

$\vdots$
$\vdots$

$$h_1 := 191.8 \cdot 1000 \cdot \frac{J}{kg} \qquad s_1 := 0.6492 \cdot 1000 \frac{J}{kg} \qquad v_1 := 0.00101 \frac{m^3}{kg}$$

Boiler inlet

Determine the thermodynamic properties at State 2 the boiler inlet.

At State 2, the pressure (P_2) is 10 megapascals and the entropy (s_2) is equal to the entropy at State 1 (s_1) because the pump is an isentropic process. In this state, the water is a compressed liquid. You only need to find the enthalpy at State 2 (h_2) from the compressed liquid table for

New propulsion system

water, because the specific volume (v_2) at State 2 is nearly the same as it is in State 1. By interpolating steam Tables you find that;

$$h_2 := 201.9 \cdot 1000 \, \frac{J}{kg}$$

Engine inlet

Determine the thermodynamic properties at State 3, the Engine inlet

At State 3, the pressure (P_3) is 10 megapascals, and the temperature (T_3) is 800 degrees Celsius. Under these conditions, the water is super heated vapor. Use these two properties to find enthalpy (h_3) and entropy (s_3) from steam Table . By interpolation, you find that;

$$h_3 := 4115 \cdot 1000 \, \frac{J}{kg} \qquad s_3 := \left[(7.408 \cdot 1000) \, \frac{J}{kg} \right] \cdot K$$

Condenser inlet

Determine the thermodynamic properties at State 4, the condenser inlet.

At State 4, the pressure (P_4) is 10 kilopascals, and the entropy (s_4) is equal to the entropy at State 3 (s_3) because the engine is an isentropic process. At the condenser inlet, the water is usaully a liquid-vapor mixture, and, in this problem, you know the saturation pressure. Use these two properties to find the enthalpy (h_4) at State 4 from steam Tables. By interpolating the steam tables, you find that;

$$h_4 := 2348 \cdot 1000 \, \frac{J}{kg}$$

Condenser inlet steam quantity

Determine the steam quality at State 4, the condenser inlet.

New propulsion system

At State 4, the pressure (p_4) is 10 kilopascals, and the enthalpy (h_4) is 2248 kilojoules/kilogram. You first find the enthalpy of both the saturated vapor (hg) and the saturated liquid (h$_f$) at State 4. Use the steam table to find h$_f$ and h$_g$;

$$h_f := 191.8 \cdot 1000 \, \frac{J}{kg} \qquad\qquad h_g := 2585 \cdot 1000 \, \frac{J}{kg}$$

Compute the quality at State 4 using the following equation:

$$x_4 := \frac{h_4 - h_f}{h_g - h_f} \qquad\qquad x_4 = 0.901$$

Pump power

Determine the pump power.

You can determine the pump power by using either of two methods. Because the pump compresses a liquid, the specific volume (v_1) doesn't change very much because liquid water is nealy incompressible substance. You can use the following equations to calculate the pump power:

$$P_1 := 10 \cdot 1000 \; Pa \quad P_2 := 10 \cdot 1000000 \; Pa \quad m_{dot} := 60 \, \frac{kg}{s} \quad v_1 = 1.01 \cdot 10^{-3} \cdot kg^{-1} \cdot m^3$$

$$W_{dot.in} := m_{dot} \cdot v_1 \cdot \left(P_2 - P_1 \right) \qquad W_{dot.in} = 6.054 \cdot 10^5 \cdot kg \cdot m^2 \cdot s^{-3}$$

$$W_{dot.in} = 6.054 \cdot 10^5 \cdot W$$

or, you can compute the power from the change in enthalpy between States 1 and 2, if these are known values as they are in this example. The result is the same

New propulsion system

$$h_2 = 2.019 \cdot 10^5 \; \bullet m^2 \bullet s^{-2} \qquad h_1 = 1.918 \cdot 10^5 \; \bullet m^2 \bullet s^{-2}$$

$$W_{dot.in.1} := m_{dot} \cdot \left(h_2 - h_1 \right) \qquad W_{dot.in.1} = 6.06 \cdot 10^5 \; \bullet kg \bullet m^2 \bullet s^{-3}$$

Engine power

Determine the engine power.

The engine power is calculated from the change in enthalpy from States 3 to 4:

$$h_3 = 4.115 \cdot 10^6 \; \bullet m^2 \bullet s^{-2} \qquad h_4 = 2.348 \cdot 10^6 \; \bullet m^2 \bullet s^{-2}$$

$$W_{dot.out} := m_{dot} \cdot \left(h_3 - h_4 \right) \qquad W_{dot.out} = 1.06 \cdot 10^8 \; \bullet kg \bullet m^2 \bullet s^{-3}$$

$$W_{dot.out} = 1.06 \cdot 10^8 \; \bullet W$$

Steam generator

Determine the heat input from the steam generator.

The heat input is calculated from the change in enthalpy from States 2 to 3:

$$h_3 = 4.115 \cdot 10^6 \; \bullet m^2 \bullet s^{-2} \qquad h_2 = 2.019 \cdot 10^5 \; \bullet m^2 \bullet s^{-2} \qquad m_{dot} = 60 \bullet kg \bullet s^{-1}$$

$$Q_{dot.in} := m_{dot} \cdot \left(h_3 - h_2 \right) \qquad Q_{dot.in} = 2.348 \cdot 10^8 \; \bullet kg \bullet m^2 \bullet s^{-3}$$

$$Q_{dot.in} = 2.348 \cdot 10^8 \; \bullet W$$

Heat rejected

Determine the heat rejected by the condenser.

The heat rejected is calculated from the change in enthalpy from States 4 to 1:

New propulsion system

$$m_{dot} = 60 \cdot kg \cdot s^{-1} \qquad h_4 = 2.348 \cdot 10^6 \cdot m^2 \cdot s^{-2} \qquad h_1 = 1.918 \cdot 10^5 \cdot m^2 \cdot s^{-2}$$

$$Q_{dot.out} := m_{dot} \cdot \left(h_4 - h_1 \right) \qquad Q_{dot.out} = 1.294 \cdot 10^8 \cdot kg \cdot m^2 \cdot s^{-3}$$

$$Q_{dot.out} = 1.294 \cdot 10^8 \cdot W$$

Reciprocating (piston) steam engine

If you are used to typical horsepower ratings such as the way manufacturers rate gas engines, you're in for a shock here. A safe bet is to figure one steam horsepower equals 3 gas engine horsepower. The truth is that one horsepower equals raising 33,000 pounds one foot in one minute or 550 pounds one foot in one second. Period. That's why we call steam "honest horsepower." Generally speaking, 750 watts equals one horsepower so 1000 watts is roughly 1.34 horsepower. In real life, you are going to need at least 2 or more horsepower as there are inefficiencies in all systems.

PLAN

So, how do you figure the horsepower of a steam engine? The standard horsepower formula in reciprocating (piston) steam engines is called **PLAN**. That stands for multiplying together:

> P = pressure (average or mean)
> L = length of stroke in feet
> A = surface area of the piston in inches
> N = number of revolutions per minute (rpm)

For example, if an engine has a 2 inch piston and a 3 inch stroke running at 1000 rpm and a 100 pound average or "mean" pressure. The area of piston (A) = 3.1415 r^2 = 3.1415 x 1 x 1 = 3.1415 square inches. The stroke (L) is 3 inches so converting to feet = 3 / 12 = 0.25 ft. The pressure (P) is 100 and the rpm (N) is 1000 so 100 x 0.25 x 3.1415 x 1000 / 33,000 = 2.37 hp.

Reciprocating engines

Reciprocating engines are the method of choice in applications of steam up to 100 horsepower. At common pressures, enormous torque can be achieved delivering a lot of power from a small, practical engine. A lot of torque means a slow, silent, and even a direct connection to the task. There is no need for high rpm, multiple gears,

New propulsion system

and their resulting noise.

Reciprocating, or piston, engines are easy to build. Their slow speed and simple design increase longevity.

In a reciprocating engine, the front port is exposed to steam chest pressure allowing the steam to enter the cylinder and start to drive the piston. A valve then starts to travel forward and will soon cut off the steam admission from the front port and expose the rear port.

The piston will continue to the end of its piston continues forward. The valve will soon cover the rear port and expose the front port to begin the process all over again.

The timing of the eccentric cam driver valve is important, which drives the valve back and forth, and its relation to the crank journal which is connected to the piston rod via the crosshead. The design of the engine includes simple adjustment features to ensure the correct timing is used.

Sizing the heat exchanger system

A steam car is rated by it's boiler's steaming capacity. Therefore, size, weight, and performance of conventional condensers and boilers for steam powered cars should be analytically investigated. Fan power is presented over a range of design and operating variables such as heat-exchanger size, heating rate, and ambient air temperature. It is found that practical condensers are about four or five times the size of conventional automobile radiators.

Boiler size is not necessarily large -100-lb (45-kg) boilers are possible for 4000-lb (1815-kg) passenger cars. The weight and fuel economy of a complete propulsion system are estimated to be quite comparable to today's internal-combustion systems.

An analytic examination of conventional condensers and boilers for a hypothetical 4000-pound (1815-kg) steam-powered passenger car is made to determine their size, weight, and required fan power. A single fin-and-tube condenser configuration is examined over a range of frontal area, depth, heat-transfer rate, ambient air temperature, and condensation temperature.

The boiler is assumed to be a once-through helix configuration. Variations in the tube diameter, tube spacing, boiler diameter, and combustion gas inlet and exit temperatures are considered. For both heat exchangers, emphasis is focused on the tradeoff between exchanger size and fan power requirements. A total propulsion system model is employed to study the interaction between the thermodynamic parameters and the heat-exchanger parameters.

The model is for a hypothetical 4000-pound (1815-kg) passenger car with 175 shaft horsepower (130 kW). .The performance of this car (e. g., acceleration and top speed) is comparable to today's typical passenger car of the same weight.

Condenser fan power is found to be quite low (under 1hp (0.7 kW)) at most operating conditions. However, condenser fan power

New propulsion system

requirements are very large (over 50 hp (37 kW)) under peak-power or hot-day conditions unless the condenser is four or five times larger than a conventional automobile radiator or the condensation temperature is temporarily increased at such times. Boiler weight could be of the order of 100 pounds (45 kg) and the volume about 1.6 cubic feet (0.045 m ^{3}), not including the burner, blower, and control assemblies.

The total steam propulsion system could be designed to weigh approximately the same as a conventional automobile propulsion system. The overall fuel cost would be no greater, and perhaps less, than today's average car.

The main concern with cycle analysis is the energy conversion efficiency of the device. This is called thermal efficiency and is defined as

$$\eta_{th} = \frac{\text{Work of engine - Pump work}}{\text{Heat added}} = \frac{(H_2 - H_3) - (H_1 - H_4)}{H_2 - H_1} \tag{1}$$

(All symbols are defined in appendix A.) In this study the assumed known variables are the boiler outlet temperature and' pressure and the condensing steam temperature. This allows H_a, H_{Q1}, and H_4 to be determined from steam tables. The engine work is determined by assuming an engine expansion efficiency qe as follows:

$$H_2 - H_3 = (H_2 - H_{3'})\eta_e \tag{2}$$

The pump work is closely approximated by

$$H_1 - H_4 = \frac{v(p_1 - p_4)}{\eta_{pump}} \tag{3}$$

where η_{Pump} is the pump efficiency and p1 is taken to be the same as

New propulsion system

p_2. The heat added may be found by solving the last two equations for $H_2 - H_1$.

Propulsion System Model

$$P_b + P_{pump} = P_e + P_c \qquad (4)$$

and the thermal efficiency may be rewritten

$$\eta_{th} = \frac{P_e - P_{pump}}{P_b} \qquad (5)$$

Only part of the engine power appears as useful shaft power since friction is present within the engine, the clutch, and the power shafting devices. The mechanical efficiency accounts for this:

$$P_{sh} = \eta_m P_e \qquad (6)$$

The useful shaft power is applied to the wheels, the condenser fan, the boiler blower, the water pump, and the other accessories. Thus,

$$P_{sh} = P_{wh} + P_{fan} + P_{bl} + P_{pump} + P_{acc} \qquad (7)$$

Eliminating Psh and Pe by combining and rearranging the last three equations leads to the expression for the boiler power:

$$P_b = \frac{P_{wh} + P_{fan} + P_{bl} + P_{acc} + (1 - \eta_m)P_{pump}}{\eta_m \eta_{th}} \qquad (8)$$

The water flow rate follows immediately:

$$\dot{m}_w = \frac{P_b}{H_2 - H_1} \qquad (9)$$

The condenser power may then be calculated from

New propulsion system

$$P_c = \dot{m}_w(H_3 - H_4) \tag{10}$$

To calculate overall powerplant efficiency it must be realized that not all the fuel energy expended in the boiler is used to heat water. Some is wasted in the boiler exhaust gases. The boiler efficiency qb is the fraction of fuel energy transferred to the water and may be calculated with equation (B61)

The energy delivered to the boiler blower is recovered since it transfers this energy to the incoming air, and from the air it is transferred to the water in the boiler. Thus the total power delivered to the boiler water is

$$P_b = \eta_b P_{fuel} + P_{bl}$$

Hence,

$$P_{fuel} = \frac{P_b - P_{bl}}{\eta_b}$$

The overall powerplant efficiency is defined as the ratio of useful work to the fuel energy. Using this definition and the previous relation yields

$$\eta_{over} \equiv \frac{P_{wh}}{P_{fuel}} = \frac{P_{wh}\eta_b}{P_b - P_{bl}} \tag{11}$$

The rate of change of distance with volumetric fuel flow (i. e., the instantaneous gas mileage) is simply

$$\text{Instantaneous gas mileage} = \frac{\mathcal{V}}{\left(\dfrac{\dot{m}}{\rho}\right)_{fuel}} = \frac{\mathcal{V}}{\left(\dfrac{\rho^h{}_{fuel}}{P}\right)_{fuel}} \tag{12}$$

The actual gas mileage experienced by a driver would be calculated by

New propulsion system

averaging this expression over an appropriate driving cycle.

The preceding set of equations describes the energy flow model. A block diagram summary of this model is shown in figure .

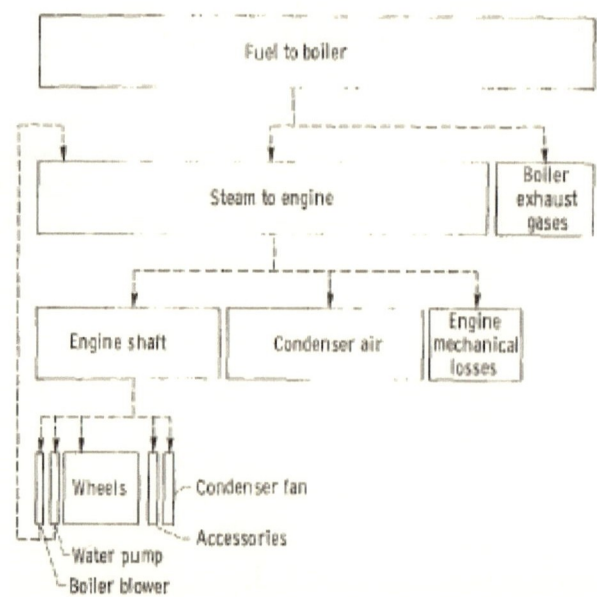

Illustration 48: This diagram shows where the original energy contained in the fuel is dissipated. Note that the energy supplied to the water pump and boiler blower is returned to the working fluid

The original energy contained in the fuel is dissipated. Note that the energy supplied to the water pump and boiler blower is returned to the working fluid. The component assumptions are as follows:

(1) Mechanical efficiency, n_m, = 0.92
(2) Engine expansion efficiency at rated power, $n_e = 0.70$
(3) Water pump efficiency, $n_{pump} = 0.50$
(4) Accessory power, Pacc = 2 hp (1.5 kW)

New propulsion system

(5) Fuel density, ρfuel = 50 lb/ft3 (800 kg/m3)
(6) Fuel heating value, hfuel = 18 500 Btu/lb (43 000 kJ/kg)

The wheel power overcomes tire friction resistance, aerodynamic drag, gravity while climbing hills, and inertia while accelerating. The gravity force is

$$F_{grav} = W_{car} \sin \beta \approx W_{car} \tan \beta = W_{car}(grade) \qquad (13)$$

where β is the angle between the road and horizontal, and its tangent is commonly referred to as "percent grade. " The tire force is

$$F_{tire} = C_{fr} W_{car} \cos \beta \qquad (14)$$

The aerodynamic resistance is given by

$$F_{aero} = \frac{1}{2} \rho v^2 C_D S \qquad (15)$$

Finally, the wheel power for unaccelerated motion is given by

$$P_{wh} = (F_{tire} + F_{aero} + F_{grav}) v = \left(C_{fr} W_{car} \cos \beta + \frac{1}{2} \rho v^2 C_D S + W_{car} \sin \beta \right) v \qquad (16)$$

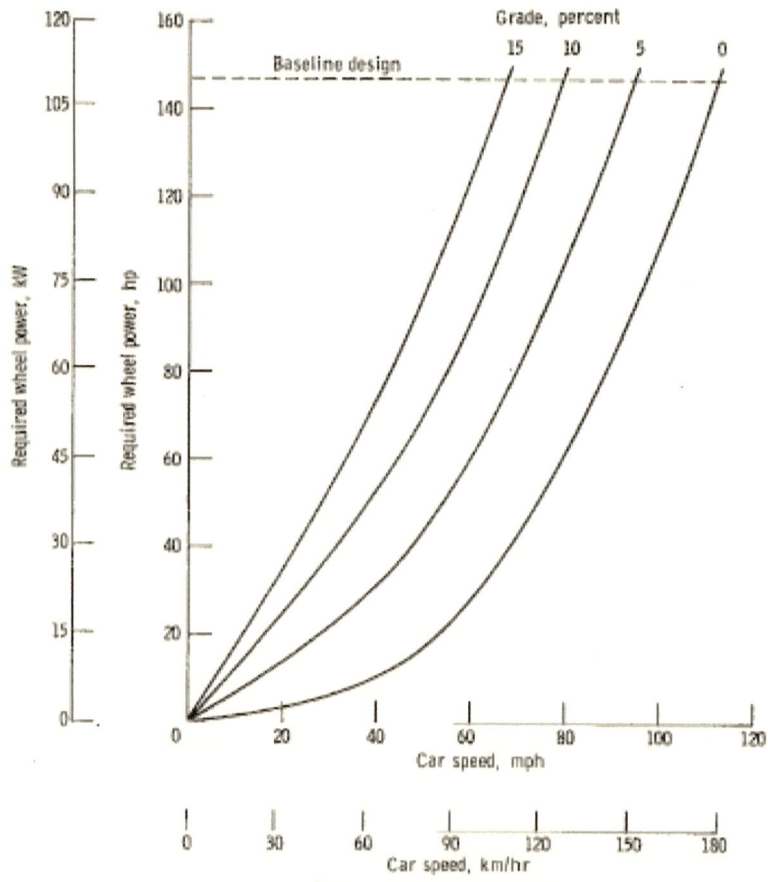

Figure 5. - Required wheel power for passenger car. Steady motion; no wind; car weight, 4000 pounds (1815 kg); frontal area, 24 square feet (2.23 m²); drag coefficient, 0.45.

Illustration 49: Required wheel power for passenger car. Steedy motion; no wind;car weight; 4000 pounds (1815 kg); frontal area, 24 square feet (2.23 m^2); drag coefficient, 0.45.

This relation is plotted in figure for CD and Cfr values based on reference 14 data and S = 24 square feet (2.23 m2). Both car speed and grade have a strong influence on wheel power. At low speeds on a level road, tire friction predominates; but above 60 miles per hour (100 km/hr), air drag predominates as a cubic function of speed.

Determine Condenser size

A single condenser configuration was examined. This flat tube and ruffled fin design is shown in sketch. A detailed description may be found in under the

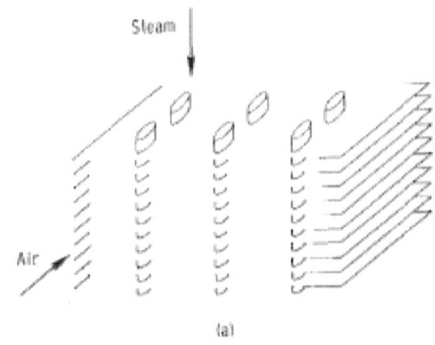

Illustration 50: flat tube and ruffled fin design is shown in sketch

designation 11.32-737-SR. Since the steps involved in the heat-transfer calculations are conventional but tedious, the procedure is only touched upon here.

Knowing the dimensions of a typical car makes it convenient to assume a condenser size and then proceed to calculate the fan power required under various operating conditions. By choosing the condenser frontal area and depth, the ambient air temperature, the condensation temperature, and the steam flow rate, it is possible to iteratively solve for the air-side pressure drop. The fan power is easily calculated from the pressure drop and the fan efficiency (assumed to be 0.7).

The conventional log-mean rate equation is used for the heat-transfer rate. This is

$$q = UAF_G \, \Delta T_{\ell m} \tag{17}$$

where q is the overall heat-transfer rate, U is the overall thermal conductance, A is the heat-transfer area, Fc, is a flow configuration correction factor equal to 1 for the cases of counterflow, boiling, or condensing, and ATlm is the log-mean temperature difference of the air and water; U must be based on whichever area (air-side or waterside) A refers to.

The condenser is assumed to be constructed with copper fins and headers, and brass tubes. This is in accord with conventional radiator fabrication techniques. There is, however, a strong incentive to use aluminum in this application since weight and cost savings would be substantial. The weight equations are also given in appendix C.

Condenser calculations

Many of the equations and data of reference 15 are used in the condenser analysis.

Volume and Weight
The total condenser volume V, is the sum of the core volume V and the header c, cvolume Vhead. With the dimensions specified in the sketch,

New propulsion system

$$V_c = V_{c,c} + V_{head} = BZL_c + 2BZ_{head}L_c \qquad \text{(C1)}$$

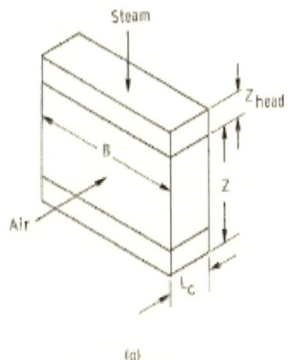

(g)

Illustration 51: The total condenser volume V, is the sum of the core volume V and the header c, cvolume Vhead. With the dimensions specified in the sketch

The condenser weight is

$$W_c = W_f + W_t + W_{head} \qquad \text{(C2)}$$

where

$$W_f \cong (1 - \sigma_w)\rho_f t_f \tau V_{c,c} \qquad \text{(C3)}$$

$$W_t = \rho_t t_t R_c \alpha_w V_{c,c} \qquad \text{(C4)}$$

$$W_{head} = \rho_{head} t_{head}(2BL + 4BZ_{head} + 4L_c Z_{head}) \qquad \text{(C5)}$$

Heat Transfer

In this study, the condenser configuration is specified and the

New propulsion system

independent variables are chosen to be the saturation temperature, the ambient air temperature, and the steam flow rate, as shown in sketch.

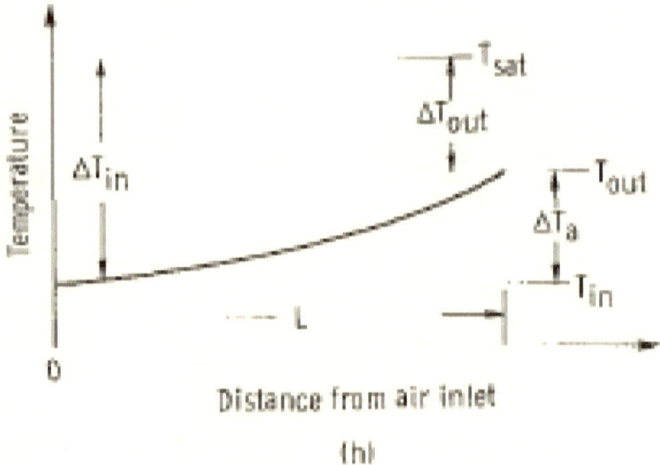

Distance from air inlet

(h)

The primary dependent variable is the fan power required to overcome the air-side pressure drop. The calculations may be performed as

$$\Delta T_{lm} = \frac{\Delta T_a}{\ln\left(\frac{\Delta T_{in}}{\Delta T_{out}}\right)} \qquad (C6)$$

$$T_{lm} = T_{sat} - \Delta T_{lm} \qquad (C7)$$

follows: Assume the air-side outlet temperature to be TSat -25' F (270 K). Calculate the log-mean temperature: Determine air property data at T lm using curve-fitted data from reference 21. These consist of the specific heat CP' the viscosity pa, the thermal conductivity ka, the Prandtl number Npr, and the specific volume v.

New propulsion system

Calculate the airflow rate per unit area:

$$\dot{m}_a = \frac{\dot{m}_w \, \Delta H_w}{C_p \, \Delta T_a} \tag{C8}$$

$$G_a = \frac{\dot{m}_a}{ZB\sigma_a} \tag{C9}$$

Calculate the air-side Reynolds number:

$$N_{R,\,a} = \left(\frac{4r_h G}{\mu}\right)_a \tag{C10}$$

Using curve-fitted data of table 23 from reference 15, determine the basic heat-transfer parameter and the friction factor:

$$\left(N_{St} N_{Pr}^{2/3}\right)_a = \text{function of } N_{R,\,a}$$

$$f_a = \text{function of } N_{R,\,a} \tag{C11}$$

The air-side heat-transfer coefficient follows immediately from the definition of Stanton number:

$$h_a = \left[\frac{\left(N_{St} N_{Pr}^{2/3}\right)}{N_{Pr}^{2/3}} C_p G\right]_a \tag{C12}$$

The fin temperature effectiveness is calculated next:

$$\eta_f = \frac{\tanh m\ell}{m\ell} \tag{C13}$$

$$m = \sqrt{\frac{2h_a}{k_f t_f}} \tag{C14}$$

Then the total surface-temperature effectiveness is

$$\eta_o = 1 - \left(\frac{A_f}{A}\right)_a (1 - \eta_f) \tag{C15}$$

The water-side flow rate per unit area is

$$G_w = \frac{\dot{m}_w}{B L_c \sigma_w} \tag{C16}$$

from which the water-side Reynolds number may be found

$$N_{R,w} = \left(\frac{4 r_h G}{\mu}\right)_w \tag{C17}$$

The water-side heat-transfer coefficient is calculated from equation (13-4) of reference 26 for laminar condensate films:

$$h_w = 1.47 \left(\frac{\mu_w}{k_w^3 \rho_w^2 g}\right)^{-1/3} \left(N_{R,w}\right)^{-1/3} \times 1.28 \tag{C18}$$

where the factor 1.28 is appended as recommended in reference 26.

Calculate the overall conductance per unit air-side area:

$$\frac{1}{U_a} = \frac{1}{\eta_o h_a} + \frac{1}{\left(\frac{\alpha_w}{\alpha_a}\right) h_w} + \frac{1}{\left(\frac{\alpha_w}{\alpha_a}\right) h_{sc}} + \frac{t_t}{\left(\frac{\alpha_w}{\alpha_a}\right) k_t} + \frac{t_t}{k_p} \tag{C19}$$

where the water-side scale deposit coefficient hsc is assumed to be 500 Btu per hour per square foot per OF (2830 W/(m 2)(K)),the air-side paint and dirt thickness tP is assumed to be 0.001 inch (0.0025 cm), and the conductivity kP is assumed to be 0.75 Btu per hour per square foot per OF per foot (130 W/(m)(K)) (ref. 27).

Calculate a new air outlet temperature from the basic heat-transfer equation as follows:

$$q = U_a A_a \, \Delta T_{lm} \tag{C20}$$

Also,

$$q = \dot{m}_a C_p \, \Delta T_a \tag{C21}$$

Combining equations (C20) and (C21) yields

$$\Delta T_a = \frac{U_a A_a \, \Delta T_{lm}}{C_p \dot{m}_a} \tag{C22}$$

Now from the definition of ΔT_{lm} given in equation (C20),

$$T_{out} = T_{sat} - \Delta T_{out} = T_{sat} - \Delta T_{in} \, \exp\!\left(-\frac{\Delta T_a}{\Delta T_{lm}}\right) \tag{C23}$$

Substituting for ΔT_a gives

$$T_{out} = T_{sat} - \Delta T_{in} \, \exp\!\left(-\frac{\alpha_a V_c U_a}{C_p \dot{m}_a}\right) \tag{C24}$$

Where the relation A, = aaVc has been used. This value of Tout is compared to the value assumed at the beginning of this procedure. If they do not closely agree, the entire procedure is repeated with the new value of Tout. Normally, three to six iterations are sufficient to produce an accuracy of 0.01 percent.

Air-side pressure drop and fan power. -The condenser air-side pressure drop and associated fan power are calculated with the same equations, (B48) and (B56), given for the boiler. There is only one region instead of three, and equation (B50) is used to determine the mean specific volume. The wall temperature To is assumed to be the condensation

New propulsion system

temperature TSat.

TABLE I. - DETAILS OF BASELINE CONDENSER

Overall dimensions:	
Width, B, ft; m	3; 0.915
Core height, Z, ft; m	2; 0.610
Header height (top and bottom), Z_{head}, in.; cm	2; 5.1
Depth, L_c, in.; cm	6; 15.2
Core volume, $V_{c,e}$, ft^3; m^3	3; 0.085
Total volume, V_c, ft^3; m^3	3.5; 0.099
Weight, lb; kg:	
Tubes (brass), W_t	57; 26
Fins (copper), W_f	66; 30
Headers (copper), W_{head}	7; 3
Total, W_e	130; 59
Air-side characteristics:	
Flow-passage hydraulic radius, $r_{h,a}$, ft; cm	0.00288; 0.0878
Heat-transfer area per unit core volume, α_a, ft^2/ft^3; m^2/m^3	270; 885
Ratio of minimum free-flow area to net frontal area, σ_a	0.780
Ratio of fin area to total area, $\left(A_f/A\right)_a$	0.845
Fin metal thickness, t_f, in.; cm	0.004; 0.01
Fin thermal conductivity, k_f, Btu/(hr)(ft)($^\circ$F); W/(m)(K)	225; 399
Fin length, 1/2 distance between tubes, l, in.; cm	0.225; 0.57
Water-side characteristics (tubes have straight sides with semicircular ends):	
Outside tube dimensions, in.; cm	0.737 by 0.10; 1.87 by 0.254
Inside tube dimensions, in.; cm	0.717 by 0.08; 1.82 by 0.203
Flow-passage hydraulic radius, $r_{h,w}$, ft; cm	0.00306; 0.0943
Heat-transfer area per unit core volume, σ_w, ft^2/ft^3; m^2/m^3	42.1; 138
Ratio of minimum free-flow area to net frontal area, σ_w	0.129
Tube metal thickness, t_t, in.; cm	0.01; 0.0254
Tube thermal conductivity, k_t, Btu/(hr)(ft^2) ($^\circ$F/ft), W/(m)(K)	60; 104
Header metal thickness, t_{head}, in.; cm	0.030; 0.0762
Condensation temperature, T_{sat}, $^\circ$F; K	212; 373
Values for design conditions[a]:	
Air outlet temperature, T_{out}, $^\circ$F; K	153; 341
Airflow, $\dot{m}_a$, lb/hr; kg/hr	80 200; 36 400
Airflow per unit free-flow area, G_a, lb/(hr)(ft^2); kg/(hr)(m^2)	17 033; 83 300
Air-side heat-transfer coefficient, h_a, Btu/(hr)(ft^2)($^\circ$F); W/(m^2)(K)	30.7; 174
Air-side friction factor, f_a	0.0229
Air-side pressure drop, $\Delta p/p_1$	0.0103
Fan power, P_{fan}, hp; kW	17; 12.6
Water flow, $\dot{m}_w$, lb/hr; kg/hr	1463; 664
Water flow per unit free-flow area, G_w, lb/(hr)(ft^2); kg/(hr)(m^2)	7564; 37 000
Water-side heat-transfer coefficient, h_w, Btu/(hr)(ft^2)($^\circ$F); W/(m^2)(K)	2043; 11 600
Heat-transfer rate, P_o, Btu/hr; W	1 425 000; 417 000

[a]175 shaft horsepower (130 kW) on 80° F (300 K) day.

ails of baseline condenser are shown in Table 1:Boiler calculations

Boiler calculations

Only one boiler concept was examined. It consists of a single tube wound in a spiral to form concentric coils, and rows of these spirals stacked together like a stack of donuts. The shape of the boiler is thus a cylinder with a central void space as illustrated in sketch b.

Employing monotube construction avoids complicated headers and has demonstrated safe operation. The water entering the boiler is heated to the saturation temperature in the liquid heating region. It is then vaporized in the boiling region, and the resulting steam is further heated in the superheat region. The combustion gas enters the end where the steam exits and therefore the boiler is a cross-counterflow arrangement. However, it can be accurately treated as a pure counterflow arrangement because there are many tube rows.

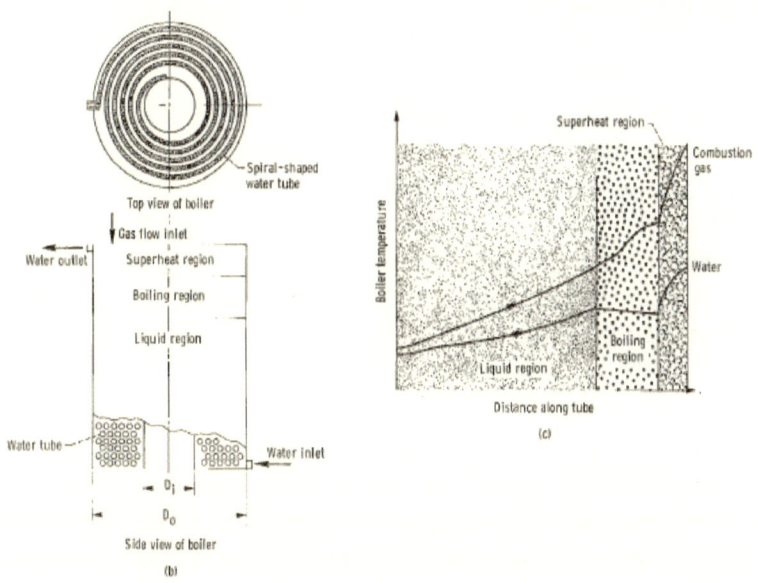

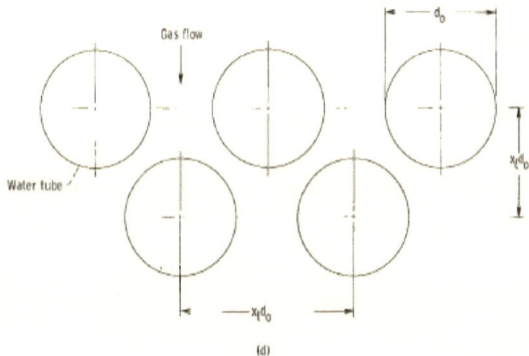

Illustration 53: Sketch illustrates the two fluid temperatures as a function of distance along the tube. Each of the three heat-transfer regions is treated separately insofar as the heat-transfer and fluid-friction calculations are concerned. The longitudinal and transverse tube spacing (see sketch) is held fixed throughout the entire boiler, although the tube pitch ratios xl and xt are varied parametrically.

Sketch illustrates the two fluid temperatures as a function of distance along the tube. Each of the three heat-transfer regions is treated separately insofar as the heat-transfer and fluid-friction calculations are concerned. The longitudinal and transverse tube spacing (see sketch) is held fixed throughout the entire boiler, although the tube pitch ratios x_l and x_t are varied parametrically. The outside tube diameter is also held fixed throughout a single design. However, the tube inside diameter is a dependent variable. It is allowed to take on three different values depending on the maximum tube-wall temperature and water pressure in each of the three regions.

This involves an iteration on the water pressure at the inlet to each region. The superheat-region

calculations are performed first, followed by the boiling-region calculations (using the superheat-region water inlet pressure as a first guess), and then the liquid-region calculations (using the boiling-region water inlet pressure as a first guess). By definition, the interface between the liquid and boiling regions is where the bulk water temperature is equal to the saturation temperature. Actually though, some subcooled boiling will occur in the liquid region because the tube-wall temperature is several degrees higher than the bulk water temperature near the interface. A sample calculation revealed that this effect is very small, however, and it was therefore ignored.

The tube material is a steel alloy known as modified 9M. It is composed of 9 percent chromium, 1 percent molybdenum, and very small amounts of columbium, vanadium, boron, nitrogen, and zirconium. This material costs about one-half as much as 316 stainless steel and yet has higher allowable stress up to 1050' F (840 K). It has already been used in SNAP-8 boilers (refs. 16 and 17) for the space program and its use for steam-car boilers appears to be an attractive application of that technology.

It should be pointed out that basically only one design configuration is being examined. There are many other configurations and concepts that might produce a better boiler. For example, finned tubing might reduce the boiler size and weight enough to offset its higher cost. Also, different flow arrangements might be more desirable. And it might be

New propulsion system

worthwhile to employ different materials, outside tube diameters, and tube spacings in the different heat-transfer regions. Variations such as these could be the subject for a more comprehensive analysis.

The details of the boiler calculations are set forth, preceded by an outline of the general calculational scheme. Many of the symbols, equations, and data are taken directly from reference 15.

Outline of Calculation Scheme

The steps of the boiler calculations are as follows:

Step A -Assume values for the following independent parameters:

6. Heat-transfer rate
7. Tube outside diameter and tube material
8. Tube spacing transverse and parallel to airflow
9. Water temperatures at the condenser outlet and boiler outlet
10. Combustion gas temperature at the boiler inlet and exhaust
11. Steam outlet pressure
12. Boiler diameter
13. Blower efficiency

Step B -Estimate values for these dependent variables:

1. Saturation water pressure in boiling region
2. Tube-wall thickness in each region

Step C -Calculate

1. Water properties at the inlet and outlet of each region
2. Water-side enthalpy change in each region
3. Airflow and airflow per unit free-flow frontal area
4. Air temperatures at boiling-region inlet and outlet
5. Air properties at the inlet and outlet of each region
6. Air-side heat-transfer coefficients and friction factors at the

New propulsion system

inlet and outlet of each region

Step D -Calculate

5. Inside tube diameter in superheat region
6. Water-side heat-transfer coefficient at superheat-region outlet
7. Superheat-region tube length and weight, based on outlet water-side and average (of inlet and outlet) air-side heat-transfer coefficients M
8. Maximum tube-wall temperature in superheat region
9. New value of tube-wall thickness, based on inlet water pressure and maximum wall temperature
10. Water-side pressure drop and inlet pressure for superheat region
11. Iterate this entire step until inlet water pressure to the superheat-region converges

Step E -Repeat step D for the boiling region and then the liquid region, using the inlet water pressure of the preceding region as a first guess.

Step F -Compute the average water pressure in the boiling region. If this value does not agree with the estimated value of saturation pressure of step B, repeat steps C through E until the saturation pressure converges.

Step G -Sum the results of the three regions to determine the total boiler weight, volume, length, number of tube rows, and number of coils in each row.

Step H -Calculate the air-side pressure drop and the required blower power.

Details of analysis

Geometry. - Some geometrical variables are calculated first. The gas-side net frontal area (see sketch b) is

$$A_{fr,g} = \frac{\pi}{4}\left(D_o^2 - D_i^2\right) \tag{B1}$$

where the boiler inside diameter Di was assumed to be 0.3 times the outside diameter Do. The minimum gas-side free-flow area $A_{c,g}$ may occur either transverse or diagonal to the gas flow. From the geometry in sketch d, the ratio of $A_{c,g}$ to $A_{fr,g}$ is

$$\left(\frac{A_c}{A_{fr}}\right)_g \equiv \sigma_g = \min\left\{\frac{x_t - 1}{x_t}, \frac{\sqrt{x_t^2 + 4x_l^2} - 2}{x_t}\right\} \tag{B2}$$

From the same sketch, the ratio of total gas-side heat-transfer area A to heat exchanger core volume $V_{b,c}$ is

$$\frac{A_g}{V_{b,c}} \equiv \alpha_g = \frac{2\pi d_o}{2x_l d_o x_t d_o} = \frac{\pi}{x_l x_t d_o} \tag{B3}$$

If L_b denotes boiler length, the gas-side flow passage hydraulic radius rh, is given
by

$$r_{h,g} \equiv L_b\left(\frac{A_c}{A}\right)_g = \left(\frac{\sigma}{\alpha}\right)_g \tag{B4}$$

Water properties. -Both water properties (ref. 20) and steam properties (refs. 13 and 21) are readily determined from tables and equations once the temperatures and/or pressures are known. The steam outlet conditions are assumed parameters. The saturation pressure is at first taken to be the same as the steam outlet pressure and later refined when the pressure drops are calculated. The water entering the boiler comes from the condenser after passing through the water pump. Hence, the specific enthalpy of boiler inlet water is just

New propulsion system

$$H_{w,\,in} = H_{w,\,c} + H_{pump} \tag{B5}$$

where HPump is given by equation (3) and HWY c is determined from the assumed condensation temperature. The water-side enthalpy change in each region follows immediately since the enthalpy is now known at the inlet and outlet of each region.

Flow rates. -The water flow rate may then be found from equation (9). The gas flow follows from an energy balance:

$$\dot{m}_g = \dot{m}_w \left(\frac{\Delta H_w}{\Delta H_g} \right) \tag{B6}$$

The gas flow per unit free-flow frontal area is simply

$$G_g = \left(\frac{\dot{m}}{\sigma A_{fr}} \right)_g \tag{B7}$$

Air temperatures. -The gas temperature at the superheat-region outlet (same as boiling-region inlet) is determined from an energy balance:

$$\Delta H_{g,\,s} = \left(\frac{\dot{m}_w}{\dot{m}_g} \right) \Delta H_{w,\,s} \tag{B8}$$

where the subscript s denotes superheat region. Since all the right-side variables are known, the gas-side superheat enthalpy change AH is determined. Furthermore, the gas inlet temperature and enthalpy are

New propulsion system

known, so by subtraction of AH from the entrance enthalpy and use of appropriate temperature enthalpy tables, the gas temperature at the superheat outlet may be calculated. The gas temperature at the liquidheating-region inlet (boiling-region outlet) is determined in a similar manner.

Air-side heat-transfer coefficients and friction factors. -All the inlet and outlet gas temperatures are now known, and the corresponding gas properties may be found by using tabular data (refs. 21 and 22). The gas-side Reynolds number is

$$N_{R,g} = \left(\frac{4r_h G}{\mu}\right)_g \tag{B9}$$

The local gas-side heat-transfer coefficients and Fanning friction factors may now be calculated from

$$h_g = \left(C_h C_p G N_{Pr}^{-2/3} N_R^{-0.4}\right)_g \qquad (300 < N_{R,g} < 15\,000) \tag{B10}$$

And

$$f_g = C_f N_{R,g}^{-0.18} \qquad (300 < N_{R,g} < 15\,000) \tag{B11}$$

where C_h and C_f are functions of x_1 and x_t as plotted in figures 33 and 34 of reference 15. The value of h at the superheat inlet is supplemented by a gas radiation term that is calculated withgthe equations and data of reference 21:

New propulsion system

$$h_r = \frac{q_r}{T_g - T_w} = \frac{\left(q_r\right)_{CO_2} + \left(q_r\right)_{H_2O}}{T_g - T_w} \tag{B12}$$

$$\left(q_r\right)_{CO_2} = \sigma^* \epsilon_w \left(\epsilon_{CO_2} T_g^4 - \epsilon'_{CO_2} T_{wall}^4\right) \tag{B13}$$

$$\left(q_r\right)_{H_2O} = \sigma^* \epsilon_w \left(\epsilon_{H_2O} T_g^4 - \epsilon'_{H_2O} T_{wall}^4\right) \tag{B14}$$

Here σ^* is the Stefan-Boltzmann constant, ϵ_W is the tube-wall emissivity (assumed to be 0. 8), e_{co2} is the carbon dioxide emissivity at the gas temperature T_g' $e'co2$ is the carbon dioxide emissivity at the tube-wall temperature T_{wall}, and similarly for the water vapor emissivities ϵ_{H20} and ϵ'_{h2O} The temperatures in equations (B13) and (B14) must be absolute temperatures. The carbon dioxide and water vapor emissivities are given in graphical form in reference 21 as a function of the product of equivalent gas layer length L_{eq} and partial pressures p_{c02} and p_{h2o}:

$$L_{eq} = 3d_o(x_t - 1) \tag{B15}$$

$$p_{CO_2} = \frac{8}{52.75 + 58.5x} \tag{B16}$$

$$p_{H_2O} = \frac{8.5}{52.75 + 58.5x} \tag{B17}$$

$$x = \frac{(a/f) - (a/f)_{st}}{(a/f)_{st}} \tag{B18}$$

The partial pressure equations (B16) and (B17) apply to units of pressure in atmospheres. The stoichiometric air-fuel ratio $(a/f)_{St}$ is 14. 9 (assuming the fuel to be C_8H_{17}). The air-fuel ratio a/f is related to the combustion gas temperature Tg by

$$a/f = \frac{h_{fuel}}{\left(\overline{H_g}\right)_{T_g} - \left(\overline{H_g}\right)_{in}} \tag{B19}$$

The tube-wall temperature Twall in the radiation calculations is not known accurately (it is estimated to be 50' C above the steam exit temperature), but this is unimportant since the radiation heat transfer is very small compared to the convective heat transfer.

Water-side heat-transfer coefficient. -The water-side Reynolds number is calculated next by guessing the tube-wall thickness tt:

$$N_{R,w} = \left(\frac{d_i G}{\mu}\right)_w \tag{B20}$$

where

$$d_i = d_o - 2t_t \tag{B21}$$

$$G_w = \frac{4}{\pi} \frac{\dot{m}_w}{d_i^2} \tag{B22}$$

The water-side heat-transfer-coefficient equation for coiled tubes is

$$h_w = \left\{ 0.023 \, \frac{k}{d_i} \, N_{Pr}^{0.4} N_R^{0.8} \left[N_R \left(\frac{d_i}{D_m} \right)^2 \right]^{0.05} \right\}_w \tag{B23}$$

The factor in brackets raised to the 0.05 power is due to coiled rather than straight tubing, according to reference 23. The mean coil diameter D_m is

$$D_m = D_o \sqrt{\frac{1}{2} \left[1 + \left(\frac{D_i}{D_o} \right)^2 \right]} \tag{B24}$$

In the boiling region, hw is multiplied by 3.6 to account for two-phase flow phenomena in accordance with graphical data in reference 24. Properties of the liquid phase are used for the boiling region.
Tube length and weight. -The average overall heat-transfer conductance for one particular region is

$$\frac{1}{U_g} = \frac{1}{\bar{h}_g} + \frac{1}{\left(\frac{d_i}{d_o} \right) h_w} + \frac{2 d_o t_t}{k_t (d_i + d_o)} \tag{B25}$$

The average gas-side heat-transfer coefficient h used in this equation is the arithmegtic average of the inlet and outlet values of .h multiplied by a correction factor givengin figure 35 of reference 15 to account for a finite number of tube rows (i.e., the value of h given above is for an infinite number of tube rows). The number of tube rows is not yet known, however, so an estimate is made initially. A better estimate is calculated later and is used on the succeeding iteration. The value of hw is taken to be the outlet value. This is not critical since h_w is of the order 50 5 and d_i/d_o is slightlygless than 1. The gas-side heat-transfer area of a region is calculated from the log-mean rate equation:

$$A_g = \frac{\dot{m}_g \, \Delta H_g}{U_g \, \Delta T_{\ell m}} \qquad\qquad (B26)$$

where

$$\Delta T_{\ell m} \equiv \frac{\left(T_g - T_w\right)_{max} - \left(T_g - T_w\right)_{min}}{\ln\left[\dfrac{\left(T_g - T_w\right)_{max}}{\left(T_g - T_w\right)_{min}}\right]} \qquad\qquad (B27)$$

For each region, the maximum temperature difference between the gas and water occurs at the gas-side inlet and the minimum difference occurs at the gas-side outlet. The tube length for each region is

$$L_t = \frac{A_g}{\pi d_o} \qquad\qquad (B28)$$

and the tubing weight is

$$W_t = \pi \rho_t t_t (d_o - t_t) L_t \qquad\qquad (B29)$$

Tube-wall temperature. -At this point it is necessary to check the tube-wall thickness estimate ma.de earlier. This requires knowing the maximum tube-wall temperature in each region. Sketch illustrates the temperature profile through the tube

New propulsion system

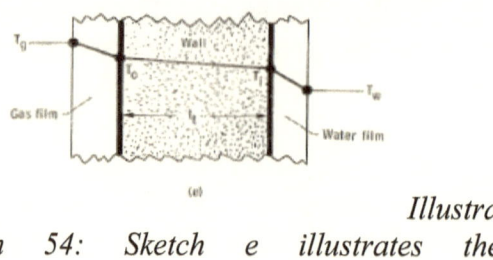

(e)

Illustration 54: Sketch e illustrates the

wall and fluid films. The tube-wall temperature may be determined from heat balance equations. Since for steady-state conditions the heat rate through the two fluid films equals the heat rate through the tube wall,

$$q = A_g h_g (T_g - T_o) = A_w h_w (T_i - T_w) = \frac{A_m k_t (T_o - T_i)}{t_t} \qquad (B30)$$

But

$$A_g = \pi d_o L_t \qquad (B31)$$

$$A_w = \pi d_i L_t \qquad (B32)$$

$$A_m = \frac{1}{2}(A_g + A_w)L_t = \frac{\pi}{2}(d_o + d_i)L_t \qquad (B33)$$

$$d_i = d_o - 2t_t \qquad (B21)$$

Substituting these four relations into the previous equation for q and rearranging yields

New propulsion system

$$\frac{q}{n L_t d_o} = h_g(T_g - T_o) = \left(1 - \frac{2t_t}{d_o}\right) h_w(T_i - T_w) = \left(1 - \frac{t_t}{d_o}\right)\left(\frac{k}{t}\right)(T_o - T_i) \qquad (B34)$$

(Gas film)   (Water film)   (Tube wall)

The gas-film and tube-wall parts of this expression may be used to solve for the inside wall temperature:

$$T_i = T_o - \frac{h_g(T_g - T_o)\left(\frac{t}{k}\right)_t}{1 - \frac{t_t}{d_o}} \qquad (B35)$$

Likewise, the gas-film and water-film parts may also be used to solve for the inside wall temperature :

$$T\, T_o = \frac{T_w + \xi T_g}{1 + \xi} \qquad (B37)$$

$$d_o$$

Finally, the last two expressions for T_i may be equated to solve for the outside tube-wall temperature:

New propulsion system

where

$$\xi = \frac{\dfrac{h_g}{h_w}}{1 - \dfrac{2t_t}{d_o}} + \frac{\left(\dfrac{t}{k}\right)_t h_g}{1 - \dfrac{t_t}{d_o}}$$

(B38)

Tube-wall thickness. -A new estimate of tube-wall thickness may now be calculated using the thin-wall.ed cylinder formula:

$$t_t = \frac{p_w d_o}{2S_{allow}}$$

(B39)

The allowable stress Sallow for modified 9M steel alloy is given in figure 2-44 of reference 16 as a function of temperature. Some representative values based on the outside wall temperature To are given in the following table:

Outside tube-wall temperature, T_o		Allowable stress, S_{allow}	
°F	K	psia	MN/m^2
700	645	22 500	155.0
900	755	19 500	135.0
1100	865	10 400	71.5
1200	920	5 800	40.0

The pressure pw in equation (B39) is initially taken to be the water outlet pressure to that particular region (e. g., 2000 psia (13. 8 MN/m^2) in the superheat region). However, the pressure drop through the tube is substantial, and this implies that the water inlet pressure must

New propulsion system

be raised in order to hold the boiler outlet steam pressure constant. Furthermore, since the superheat region accounts for only about 10 percent of the total tube length, it consists of just the last two rows of tubing (typically). Thus, the geometry is such that the maximum superheat water pressure occurs at approximately the maximum wall temperature. Therefore, both the maximum water pressure and wall temperature were used to determine the tube-wall thickness even though both conditions do not occur at exactly the same point in each region.

Water-side pressure drop. -The water-side pressure drop was estimated with the equations contained in reference 25 for straight tubes modified by a correction factor for coiled tubes (ref. 23). Specifically,

$$\Delta p_w = \left[\frac{G^2(v_\ell - v_{\ell,sat})}{g} + \frac{fG^2(v_\ell + v_{\ell,sat})L_t}{d_i} \right]_w \qquad \text{(liquid heating region)} \qquad (B40)$$

$$\Delta p_w = \left(\frac{v_v G^2}{g} r_2 + \frac{2fG^2 v_v L_t}{gd_i} r_3 \right)_w \qquad \text{(boiling region)} \qquad (B41)$$

$$\Delta p_w = \left[\frac{G^2(v_v - v_{v,sat})}{g} + \frac{fG^2(v_v + v_{v,sat})L_t}{gd_i} \right]_w \qquad \text{(superheat region)} \qquad (B42)$$

where f_w is the Fanning friction factor for single-phase water flow in a coiled tube:

$$f_w = 0.046 \, N_{R,w}^{-0.2} \left[N_{R,w} \left(\frac{d_i}{D_m} \right)^2 \right]^{0.05} \qquad (B43)$$

New propulsion system

and r_2 and r_3 are two-phase flow factors dependent on pressure and steam quality that are plotted in figures 7 and 9 of reference 25. For pw = 2100 psia (14. 5 MN/m) and steam quality equal to 1.0, r_2 = 5.664 and r_3 = 3.832.

Iterations. -

Replacing pw with $p_w + \Delta p_w$ and using the new estimate of wall thickness, the step D calculations are repeated until convergence is obtained.

The boiling-region calculations are done next using the p_w value just obtained for the superheat-region inlet. The tube-wall thickness for the boiling region is based on the maximum pressure and temperature in this region rather than being kept the same as for the superheat region.

Similarly, the liquid-region calculations are done after those for the boiling region. Thus, there are three successive iterations, one for each region.

After the calculations for all three regions are completed, the assumed saturation pressure in the boiling region is checked using the average of the calculated inlet and outlet water pressure. If the two values do not agree, the step C through step E calculations are successively repeated until convergence is obtained. This is an iteration over the entire set of the three pw iterations just discussed.

where A_g is the sum of the region areas. The boiler length is

$$L_b = \frac{4}{\pi} \frac{V_b}{D_o^2} \tag{B45}$$

and the number of tube rows (see sketch b) is

$$N_{row} = \frac{L_b}{x_l d_o} \tag{B46}$$

Boiler volume, length, and weight. -The total tube area, length, and weight are determined by summing the values of each region. The total

New propulsion system

boiler volume, including the central void, is

The number of coils per row is

$$N_{coil} = \frac{D_o\left(1 - \frac{D_i}{D_o}\right)}{2x_t d_o}$$ (B47)

The boiler weight is taken to be the total tube weight plus an allowance for the casing. The casing is assumed to consist of two 0.05-inch (0.13-cm) thick steel cylinders of diameter D_o. No weight estimate is included for the thermal insulation placed between the two casing walls, or for the controls, valves, or burner.

Gas-side pressure drop. -The gas-side pressure drop through the boiler core IS CALCULATED in each region with equation (24b) of reference 15.

$$\left(\frac{\Delta p}{p_1}\right)_g = \frac{G_g^2}{2g}\left(\frac{v_1}{p_1}\right)_g\left[(1 + \sigma^2)\left(\frac{v_2}{v_1} - 1\right) + f\left(\frac{A}{A_c}\right)\left(\frac{v_m}{v_1}\right)_g\right]$$ (B48)

New propulsion system

Here f is the average Fanning friction factor and v_m is the mean specific volume. Subscripts 1 and 2 denote gas-side inlet and outlet, respectively. The mean specific volume is

$$v_m = \frac{1}{2}(v_1 + v_2) \quad \text{(liquid and superheat regions)} \tag{B49}$$

$$v_m = \left(\frac{p_1}{\bar{p}}\right)\left(\frac{T_{lm}}{T_1}\right)v_1 \quad \text{(boiling region)} \tag{B50}$$

where

$$\bar{p} = \frac{1}{2}(p_1 + p_2) \tag{B51}$$

$$p_2 = p_1 - \left(\frac{\Delta p}{p_1}\right)p_1 \tag{B52}$$

$$v_1 = \frac{1}{X_d}\left(\frac{RT_1}{Mp_1}\right) \tag{B53}$$

$$v_2 = \frac{1}{X_d}\left(\frac{RT_2}{Mp_2}\right) \tag{B54}$$

and,

$$T_{lm} = T_o + \frac{(T_{g,\,in} - T_o) - (T_{g,\,out} - T_o)}{ln\left(\dfrac{T_{g,\,in} - T_o}{T_{g,\,out} - T_o}\right)} \tag{B55}$$

New propulsion system

There are two different equations (ref. 15) for vm because the tube-wall temperature T_0 is essentially constant in the boiling region but varies approximately linearly in the liquid and superheat regions. The density correction factor X_d for humidity and combustion products is found from data in reference 15 by assuming the ratio of water vapor to dry air is 0. 015 and the ratio of hydrogen to carbon of the fuel to be 0. 18. Initially, p_2 is estimated and then checked after the pressure drop is calculated. If the estimated value of p_2 does not agree with the calculated value, the pressure drop is recalculated with the new value of p_2. Two or three iterations usually produce an accuracy of 0.1 percent.

Blower power. -The boiler blower power is determined from

$$P_{bl} = \dot{m}_a \, \Delta H_a = \frac{\dot{m}_a C_p (\Delta T_a)'}{\eta_{bl}} = \frac{\dot{m}_a C_p T_1 \left[\left(1 + \frac{\Delta p}{p_1}\right)^{(\gamma-1)/\gamma} - 1 \right]}{\eta_{bl}} \qquad (B\,56)$$

The pressure drop is taken to be the sum of the three regional pressure drops (the burner pressure drop is neglected) and the blower efficiency q_{bl} is assumed to be 0.70.

Boiler Efficiency

Assuming that the exhaust gas is air, the conservation of energy law states that (Heat energy delivered by fuel) = (Increase in air energy) + (Increase in water energy)

or

$$\dot{m}_a (f/a) h_{fuel} = \dot{m}_a \, \Delta H_a + \dot{m}_w \, \Delta H_w \qquad (B\,57)$$

where the combustion efficiency is assumed to be 100 percent. The

New propulsion system

boiler efficiency is defined as

$$\eta_b \equiv \frac{\text{Increase in water energy}}{\text{Heat energy delivered by fuel}} = \frac{\dot{m}_w \Delta H_w}{\dot{m}_a (f/a) h_{fuel}} \tag{B58}$$

Using equation (B57) to eliminate $(\dot{m}_w/\dot{m}_a)\Delta H_w$ yields

$$\eta_b = 1 - \frac{\Delta H_a}{(f/a) h_{fuel}} = 1 - \frac{\left(H_3 - H_1\right)_a}{(f/a) h_{fuel}} \tag{B59}$$

The subscripts on the air-side enthalpy are defined in sketch f. Also, considering the conservation of energy for the burner alone,

$$\dot{m}_a (f/a) h_{fuel} = \dot{m}_a \left(H_2 - H_1\right)_a \tag{B60}$$

New propulsion system

and using this equation to eliminate $(f/a)h_{fuel}$ in equation (B59) yields

$$\eta_b = 1 - \left(\frac{H_3 - H_1}{H_2 - H_1}\right)_a \tag{B61}$$

The boiler efficiency is tabulated as follows for 80° F (300 K) ambient air temperature:

Maximum gas temperature in boiler, T_2		Exhaust gas temperature, T_3, $^\circ$F (K)			
		200 (367)	300 (422)	400 (478)	500 (533)
		Boiler efficiency, η_b			
$^\circ$F	K				
1500	1090	0.921	0.855	0.788	0.720
2000	1370	.943	.895	.847	.798
2500	1645	.956	.918	.881	.843
3000	1920	.964	.933	.903	.872

The gas tables of reference 22 were used to evaluate H_1, H_2, and H_3 as functions of the ambient, maximum, and exhaust gas temperatures, respectively..

Details of baseline Boiler are shown in Table II:

TABLE II. - DETAILS OF BASELINE BOILER

Overall dimensions:	
Outside diameter, D_o, ft; m	1.1; 0.335
Length, L_b, ft; m	1.68; 0.513
Net frontal area, $A_{fr,g}$, ft^2; m^2	0.865; 0.0804
Total volume, V_b, ft^3; m^3	1.60; 0.045
Weight, lb; kg:	
Tubing (modified 9M steel alloy)	84.5; 38.4
Casing (steel)	12.5; 5.7
Total	97.0; 44.1
Tube geometry and temperature:	
Number of tube rows, N_{row}	40
Number of coils per row, N_{coil}	6
Longitudinal pitch, x_l	1.0
Transverse pitch, x_t	1.4
Minimum distance between tubes (occurs diagonal to gas flow), in.; cm	0.11; 0.28
Total heat-transfer area, A_g, ft^2; m^2	78; 7.25
Outside tube diameter, d_o, in.; cm	0.5; 1.27
Tube-wall thickness, t_t, in.; cm	
Superheat region	0.0485; 0.123
Boiling region	0.0243; 0.0617
Liquid region	0.0253; 0.0640
Tube length, L_t, ft; m	
Superheat region	49; 15
Boiling region	83; 25
Liquid region	468; 142
Maximum wall temperature, T_o, °F; K:	
Superheat region	1079; 855
Boiling region	661; 623
Liquid region	664; 625
Tube material thermal conductivity, k_t, Btu/(hr)(ft)(°F); W/(m)(K)	16; 28.4

TABLE II. - Concluded. DETAILS OF BASELINE BOILER

Gas-side characteristics of design power[a]:

Gas flow, $\dot{m}_g$, lb/hr; kg/hr	2546; 1158
Gas flow per unit net frontal area, G_g, lb/(hr)(ft^2); kg/(hr)(m^2)	10 300; 50 400
Ratio of minimum free-flow area to net frontal area, σ_g	0.286
Ratio of heat-transfer area to core volume, α_g	53.9
Flow-passage hydraulic radius, $r_{h,g}$, ft; m	0.0053; 0.00162
Boiler efficiency, η_b	0.933
Fanning friction factor, f_a (average)	0.0535
Pressure drop, $(\Delta p/p_1)_g$	0.0466
Blower power, P_{bl}, hp; kW	2.41; 1.80
Inlet temperature, $T_{g,\,in}$, °F; K:	
Superheat region	3000; 1920
Boiling region	2311; 1540
Liquid region	1438; 1055
Outlet temperature, liquid region, $T_{g,\,out}$, °F; K	300; 422
Average heat-transfer coefficient, h_g, Btu/(hr)(ft^2)(°F); W/(m^2)(K):	
Superheat region	46.5; 263
Boiling region	50.0; 283
Liquid region	42.2; 239

Water-side characteristics at design power[a]:

Water flow, $\dot{m}_w$, lb/hr; kg/hr	1482; 674
Superheat outlet pressure, $(p_{w,\,out})_s$, psia; MN/m^2	2000; 13.8
Inlet pressure, $p_{w,\,in}$, psia; MN/m^2:	
Superheat region	2178; 15.0
Boiling region	2244; 15.5
Liquid region	2329; 16.0
Superheat outlet temperature, $T_{w,\,out}$, °F; K	1000; 810
Inlet temperature, $T_{w,\,in}$, °F; K:	
Superheat region	648; 615
Boiling region	652; 618
Liquid region	234; 386
Water inventory, lb; kg	26; 12
Heat-transfer rate, P_b, Btu/hr; W	1 900 000; 557 000
Ratio of water flow to shaft power, lb/hp-hr; kg/W-hr	8.47; 5.18

[a]175 shaft horsepower (130 kW).

APPENDIX

APPENDIX A

SYMBOLS

A	total heat-transfer area on one side of exchanger	H	specific enthalpy
		h	heat-transfer coefficient
A_c	minimum free-flow area on one side of exchanger	h_{fuel}	heating value of fuel
		k	thermal conductivity
A_f	total fin area on one side of exchanger	L_b	boiler length
		L_c	condenser depth
A_{fr}	frontal area of heat exchanger	L_{eq}	equivalent gas layer length
a/f	air-fuel ratio	L_t	boiler tube length
B	condenser width	l	effective fin length
C_D	drag coefficient of car	M	molecular weight
C_f	correlation parameter for friction outside tube banks	m	$\sqrt{2h/kt}$
		$\dot{m}$	mass flow rate
C_{fr}	friction force coefficient for car	N_{coil}	number of coils per row of boiler tubing
C_h	correlation parameter for heat transfer outside tube banks	N_{Pr}	Prandtl number, $\mu C_p/k$
C_p	specific heat at constant pressure	N_R	Reynolds number, $4r_h G/\mu$
		N_{row}	number of tube rows in boiler
D	diameter of boiler	N_{St}	Stanton number, h/GC_p
d	diameter of boiler tubing	P	power
F	force	p	pressure
F_G	flow configuration correction factor	q	overall heat-transfer rate
		R	universal gas constant
f	flow Fanning friction factor	R_c	ratio of average circumference to inside circumference of condenser tubes
f/a	fuel-air ratio		
G	mass flow rate per unit flow area		
		r_h	flow passage hydraulic radius
g	gravitational constant		

r_2, r_3	two-phase-flow friction factors	γ	specific-heat ratio
S	car frontal area	ϵ	emissivity
S_{allow}	allowable stress	ξ	defined by eq. (B38)
T	temperature	η_b	boiler efficiency
t	thickness	η_{bl}	blower efficiency
U	overall thermal conductance	η_e	engine expansion efficiency
V_b	total volume of boiler	η_f	fin temperature effectiveness
$V_{b,c}$	core volume of boiler	η_m	mechanical efficiency of engine
V_c	total volume of condenser	η_o	total surface-temperature effectiveness
$V_{c,c}$	condenser core volume		
V_{head}	condenser header volume	η_{over}	overall powerplant efficiency
$\mathscr{V}$	car speed	η_{pump}	water pump efficiency
v	specific volume	η_{th}	thermal efficiency
W	weight	μ	absolute viscosity
X_d	density correction factor for humidity	ρ	density
x	percent of excess air in burner	σ	free-flow area per unit frontal area, A_c/A_{fr}
x_l	ratio of longitudinal pitch to tube diameter	σ^*	Stefan-Boltzmann constant
x_t	ratio of transverse pitch to tube diameter	τ	fin pitch (number of fins per unit length)
		Subscripts:	
z	condenser core height	a	air
z_{head}	condenser header height	acc	accessories
α	heat-transfer area of one side of heat exchanger per unit total exchanger core volume	$aero$	aerodynamic
		b	boiler
		bl	boiler blower
		$burn$	burner
β	angle between road and horizontal	c	condenser
		car	car

e	engine	s	superheat section
f	condenser air-side fins	sat	saturation
fan	condenser fan	sc	scale on water-side
fuel	fuel	sh	engine shaft
g	gas-side of boiler	st	stoichiometric
grav	gravity	t	tubes (boiler or condenser,
head	condenser headers		as specified)
i	inside	tire	tire
in	inlet	v	vapor
l	liquid	w	water
lm	log-mean	wall	wall
m	mean value	wh	car wheels
max	maximum	1	entrance
min	minimum	2	exit
o	outside	3	condenser entrance
out	outlet	4	condenser exit
p	paint and dirt on air side		
pump	water pump	Superscripts:	
r	radiation	−	average
		'	ideal

Drawings

"The devil is in the Details"

Don't forget to visit the website blog for updates and detail engineering drawings

https://davedelgado.webs.com/

The purpose of the drawings herein are to include details of unique processes, when essential to design and manufacturing; detail performance ratings; dimensional and toerance data; critical manufacturing assembly sequences; toleranced input and output parameters; schematics; mechanical and electrical connections; physical characteristics; including form and finishes; details material identification; inspection; test and evaluation criteria; necessary calibration information; and quality control data as applicable.

Many drawings show pictorial information by means of solid model in place of coventional orthographic line-drawings. It is hoped to be useful in acquainting a person(s) with or without engineering background, with the item as to its assembly, function,installation, etc.

New propulsion system

New propulsion system

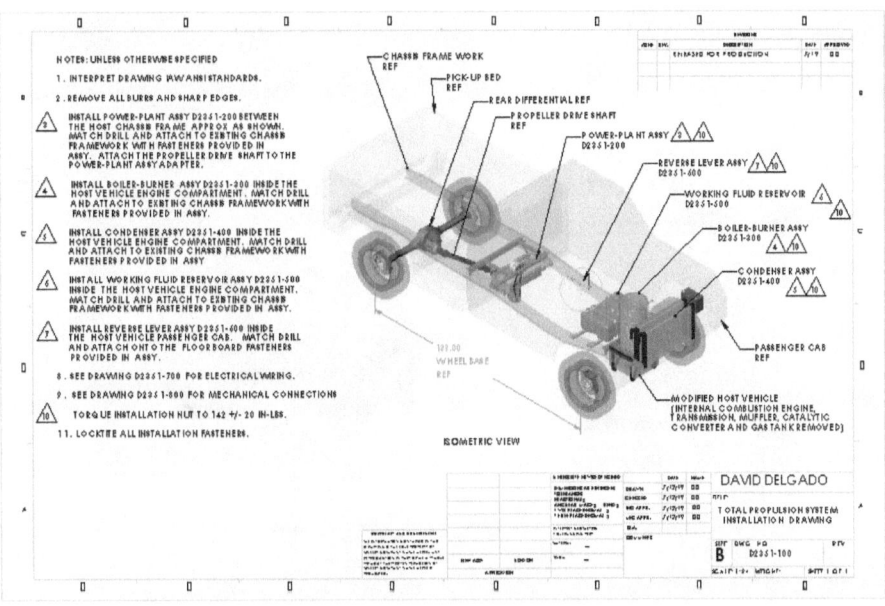

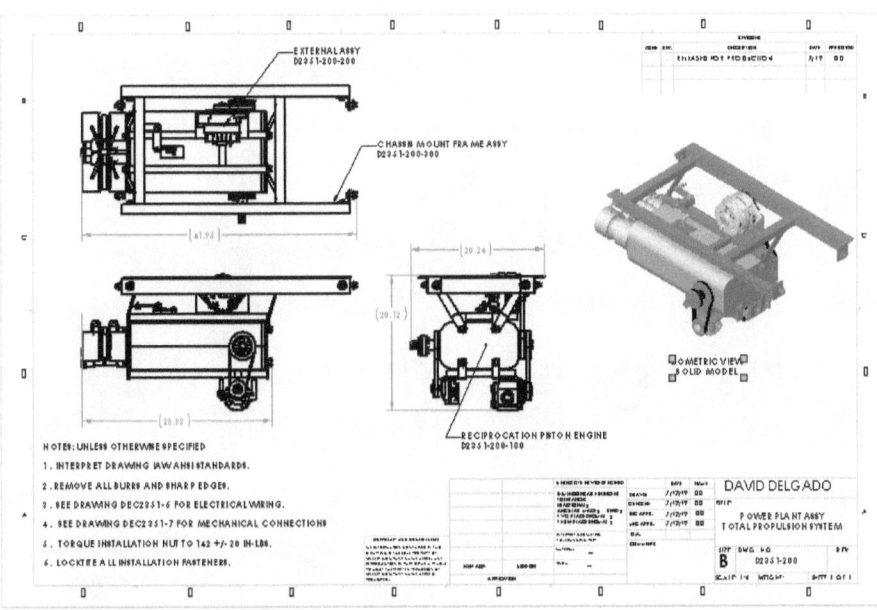

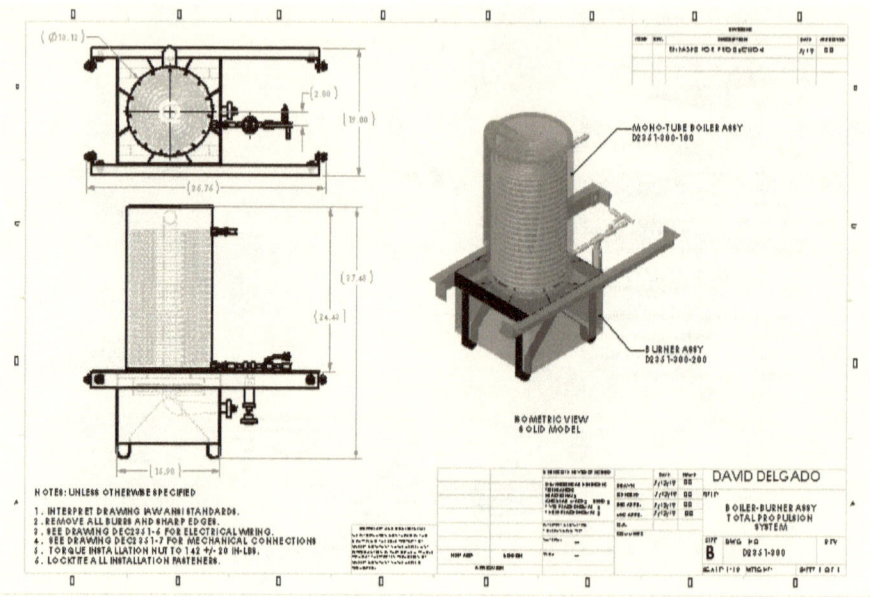

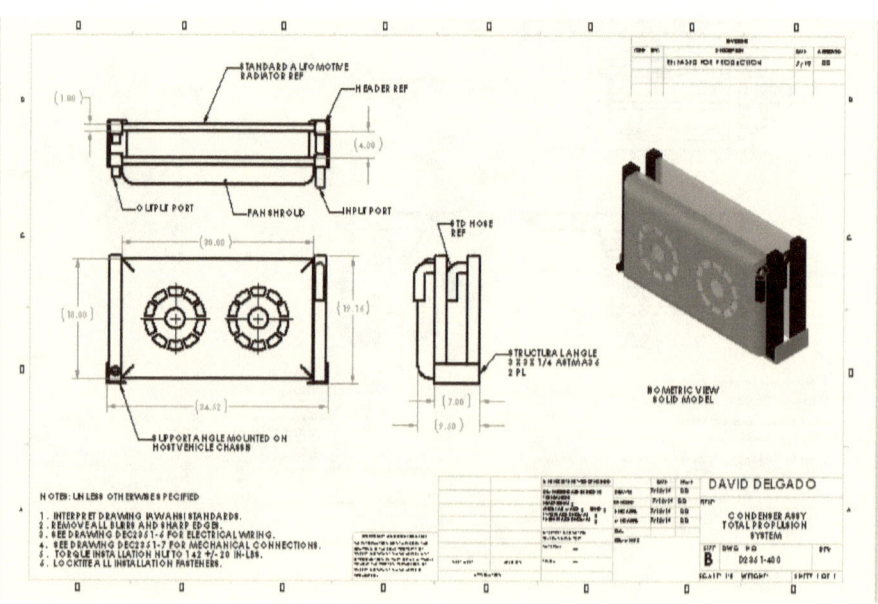

New propulsion system

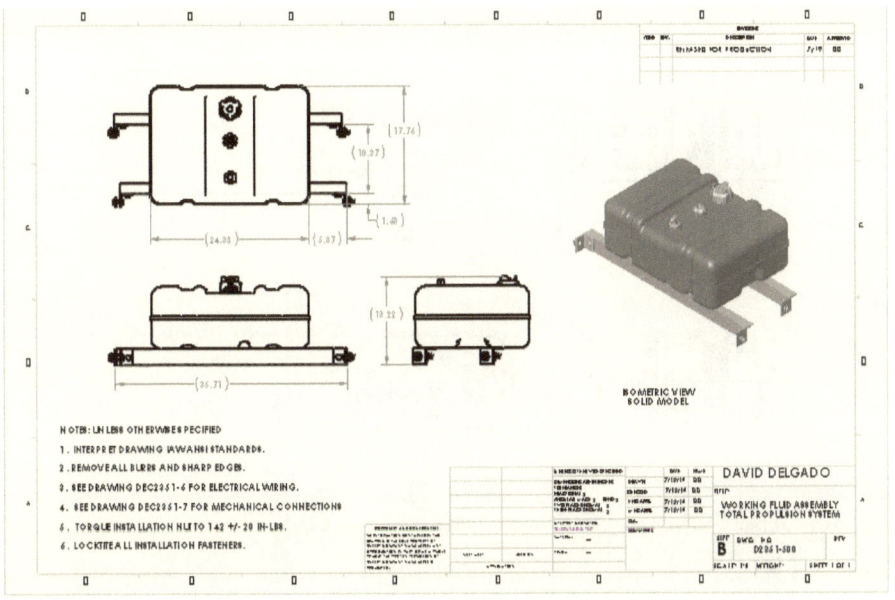

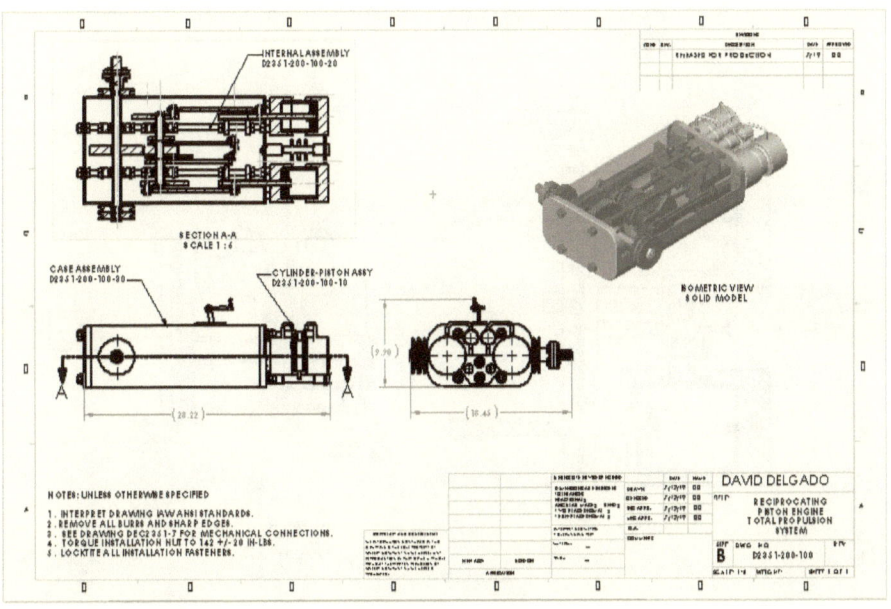

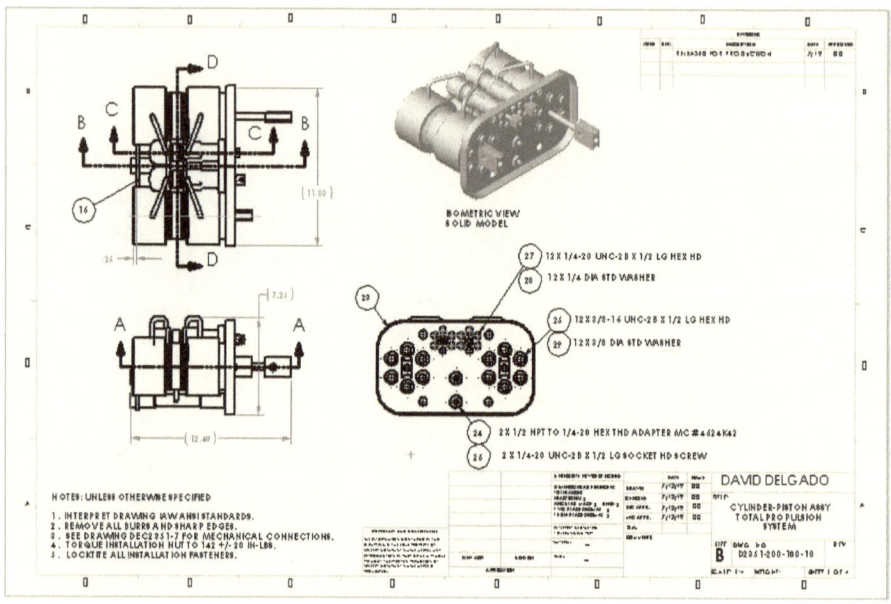

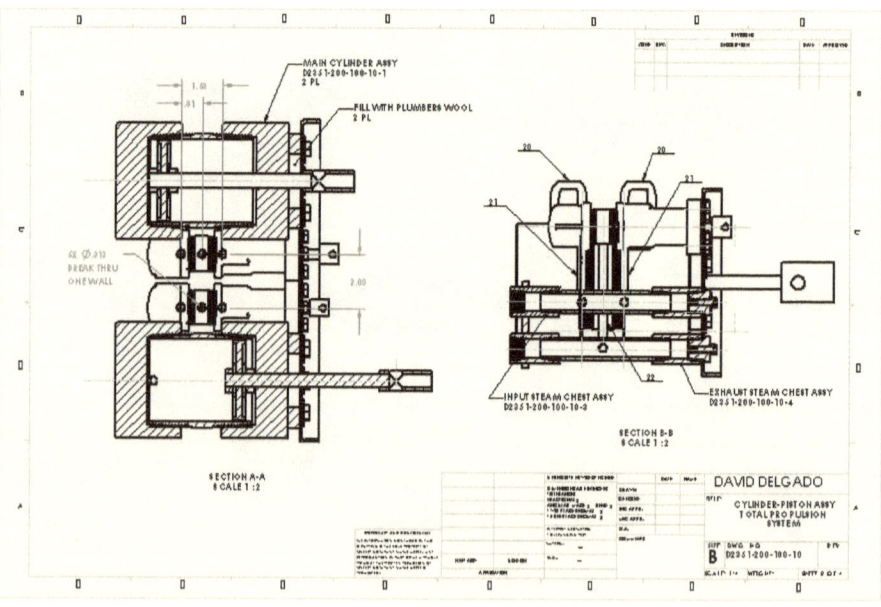

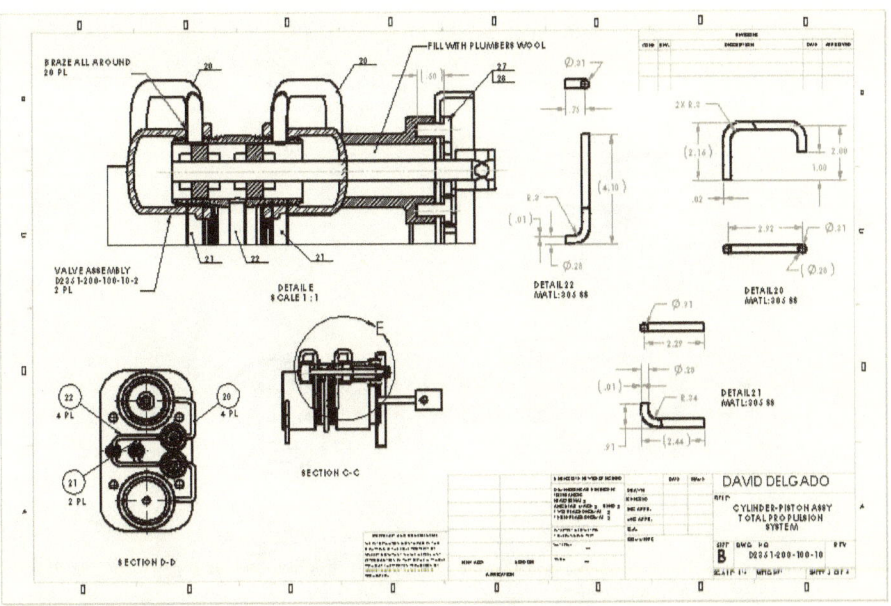

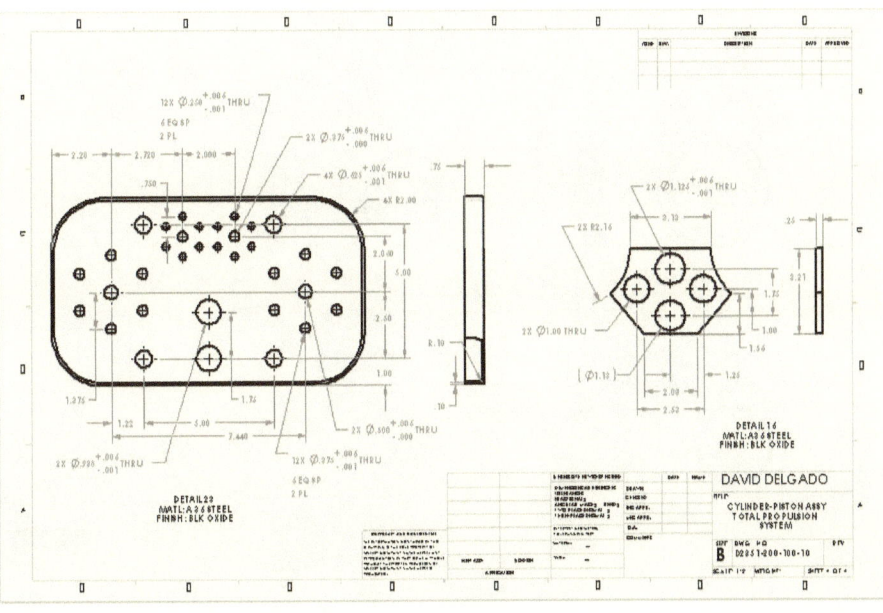

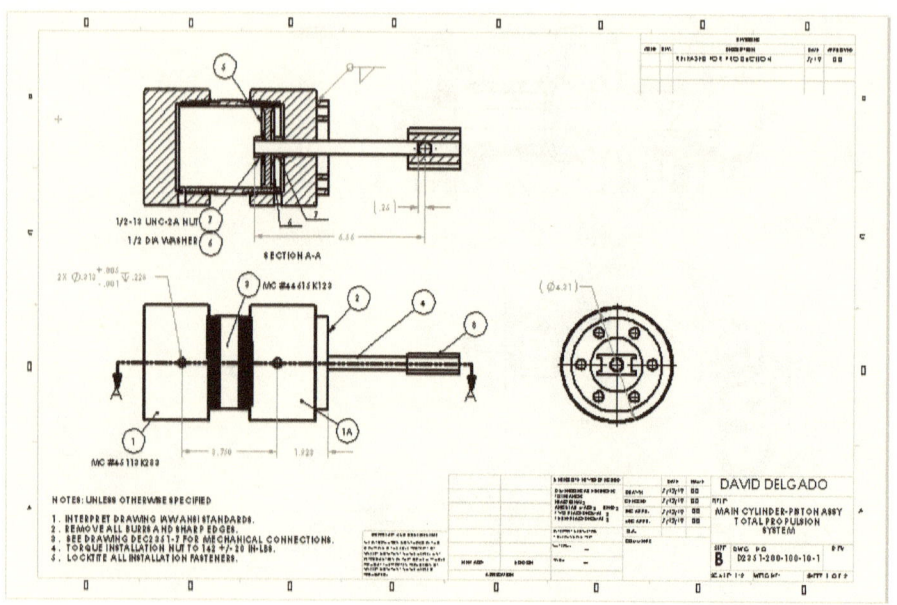

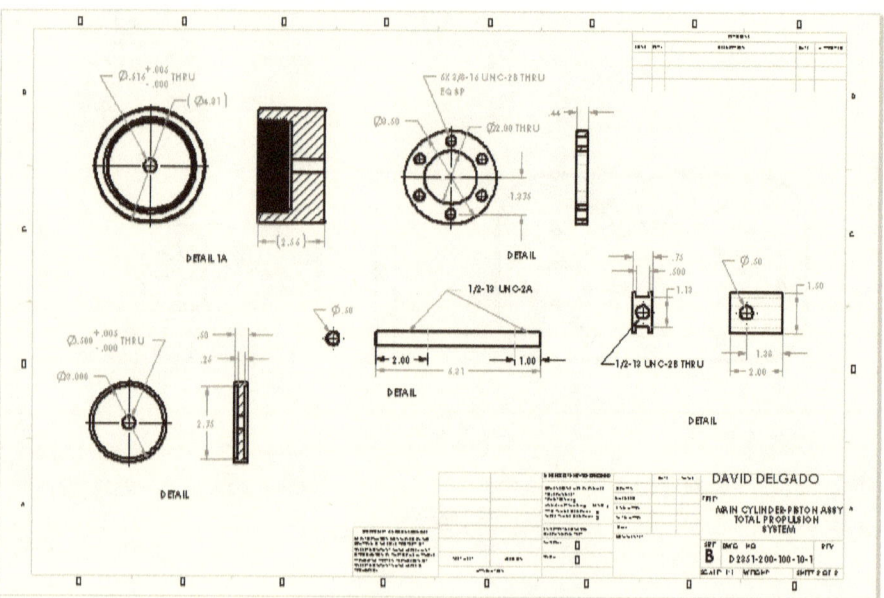

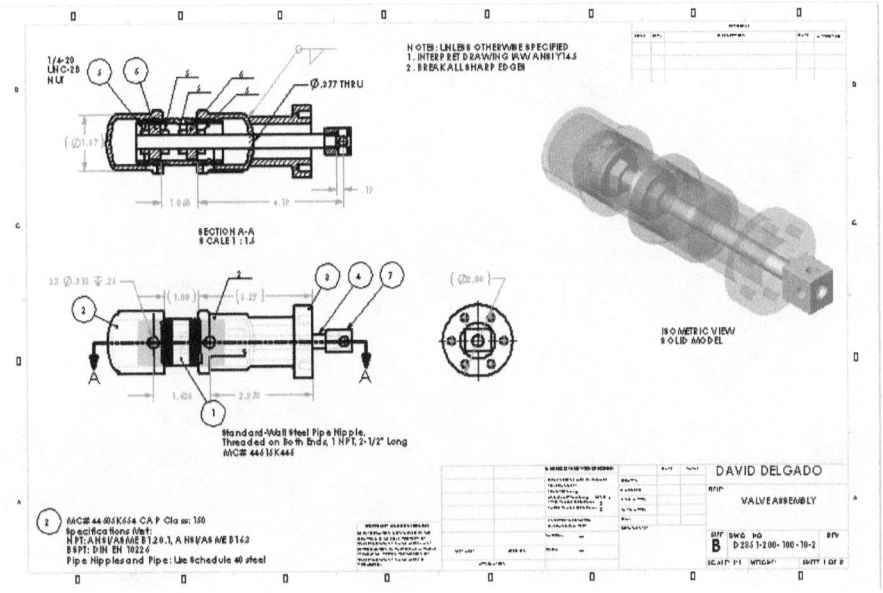

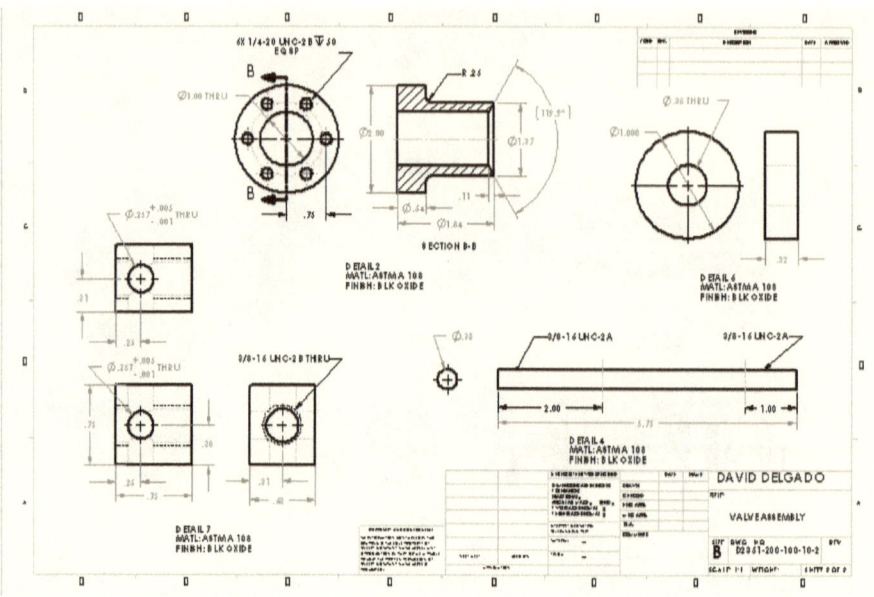

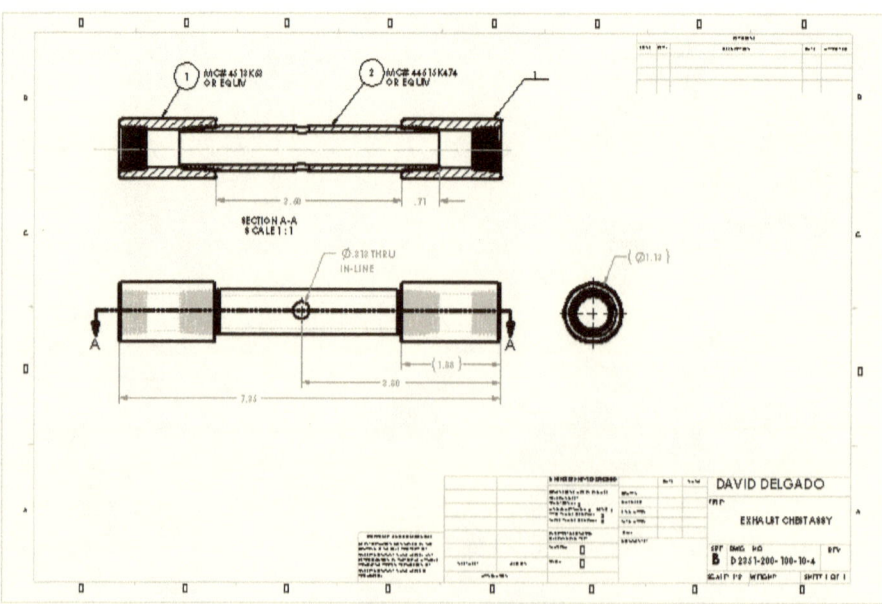

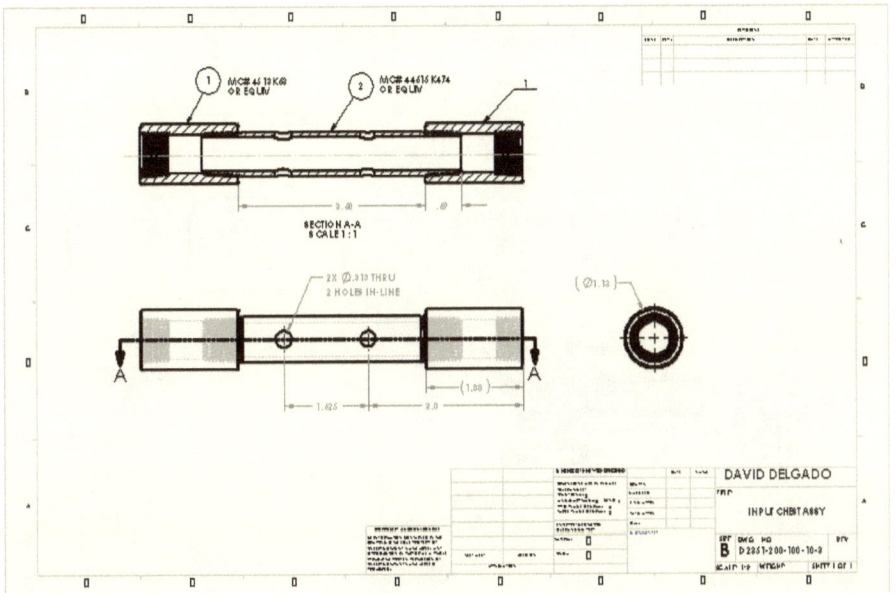

New propulsion system

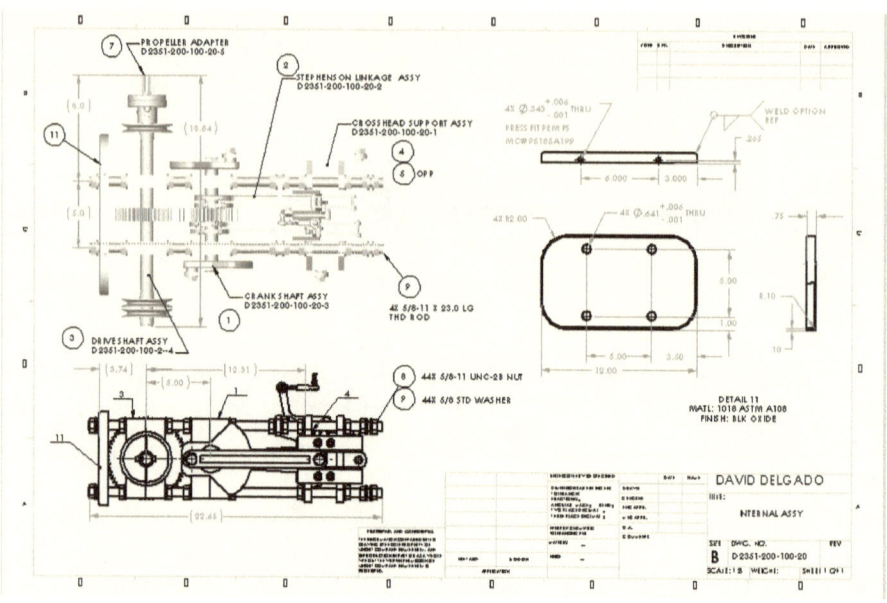

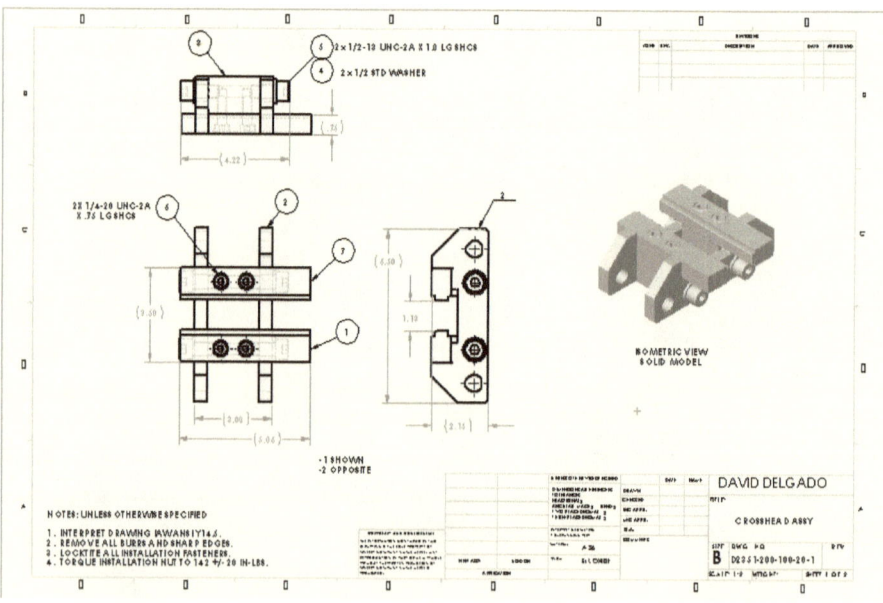

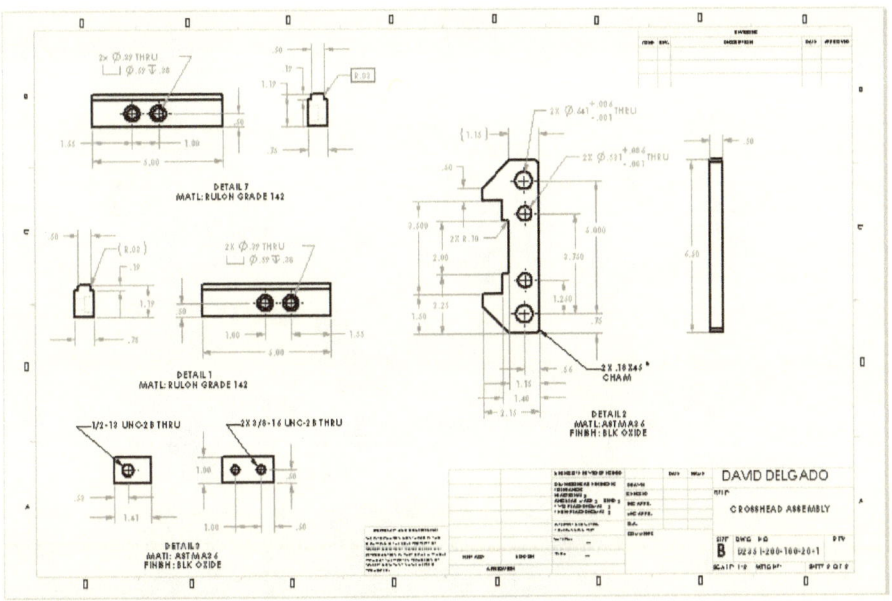

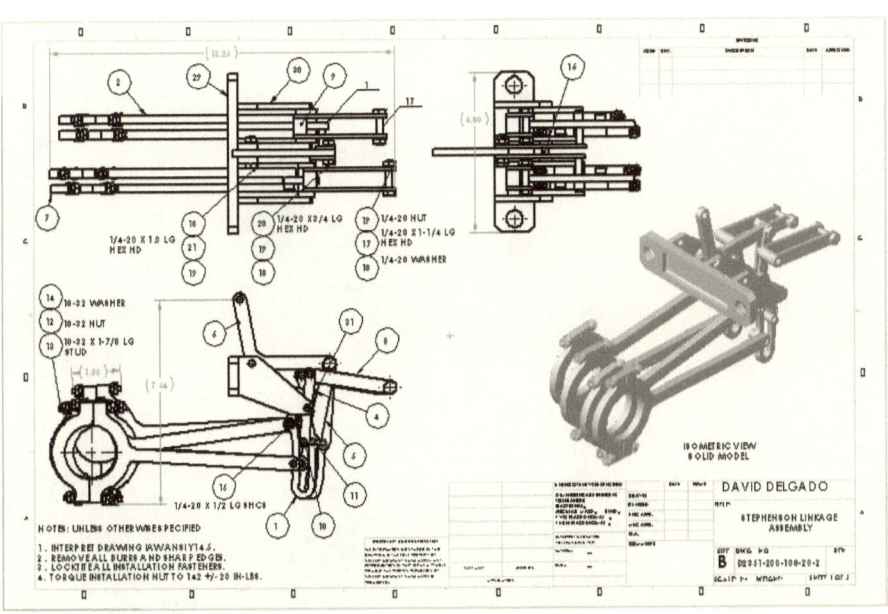

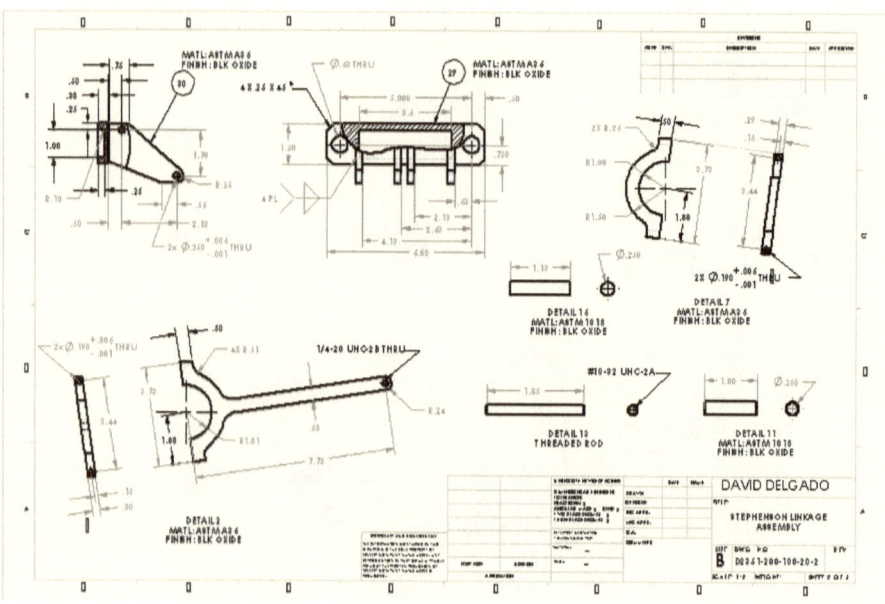

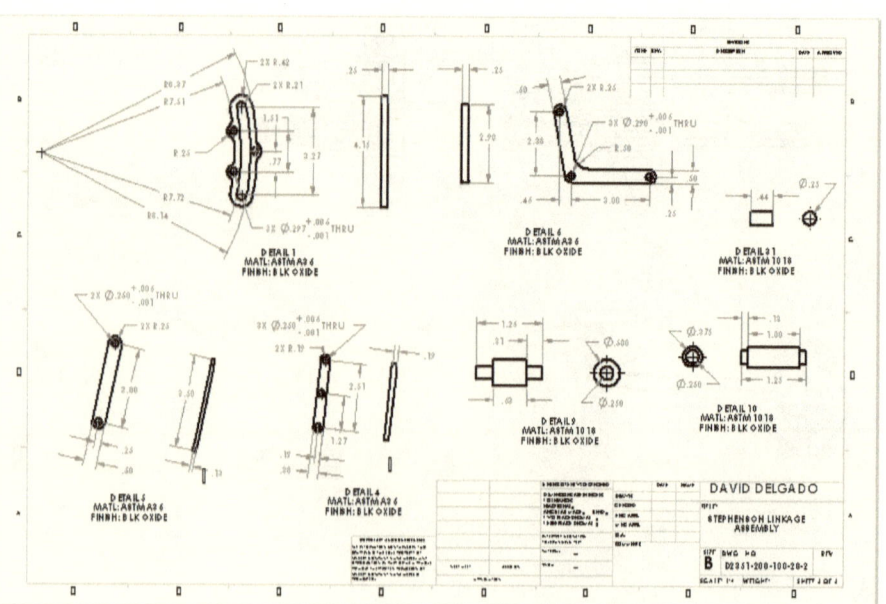

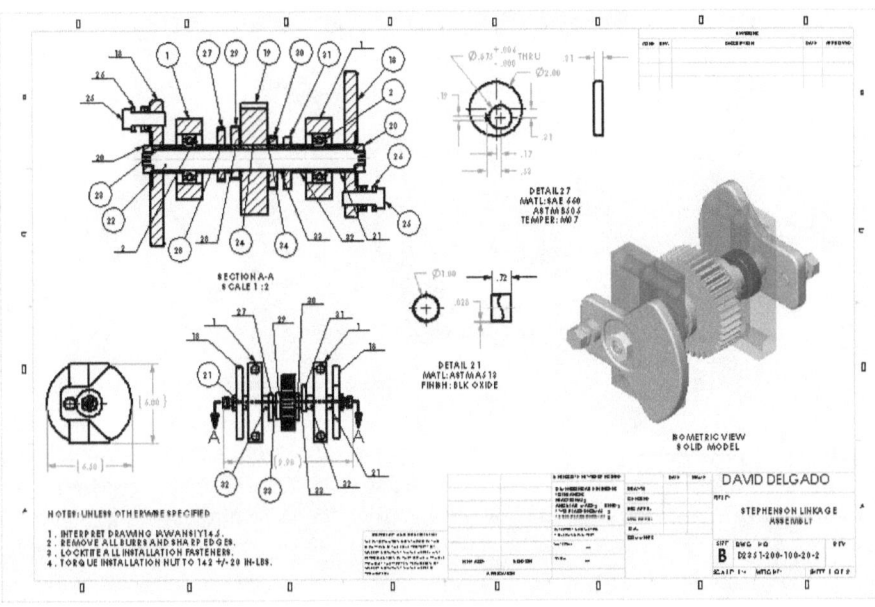

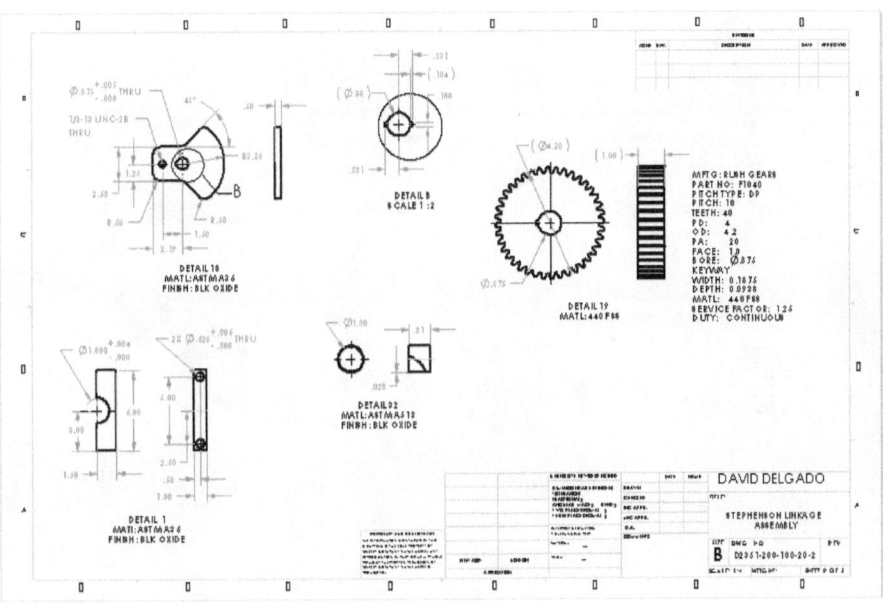

New propulsion system

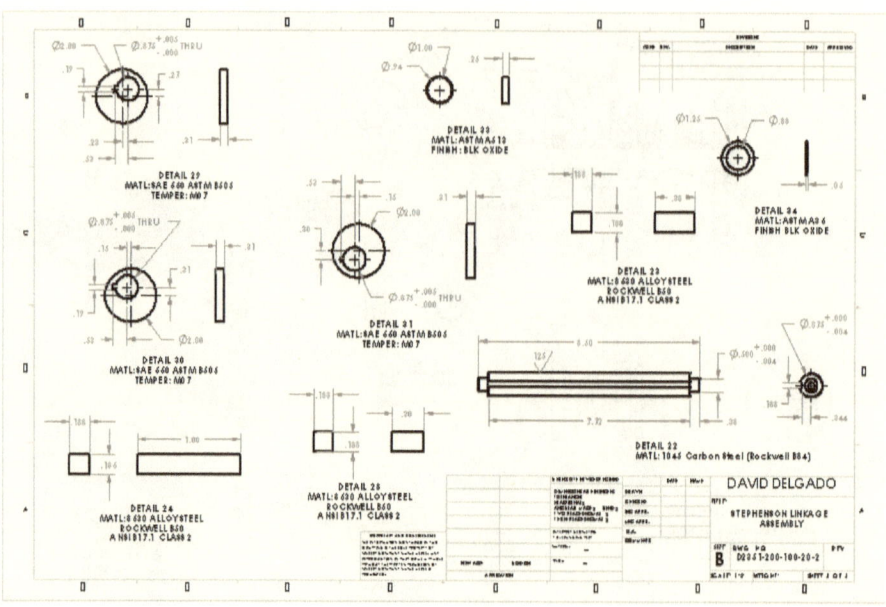

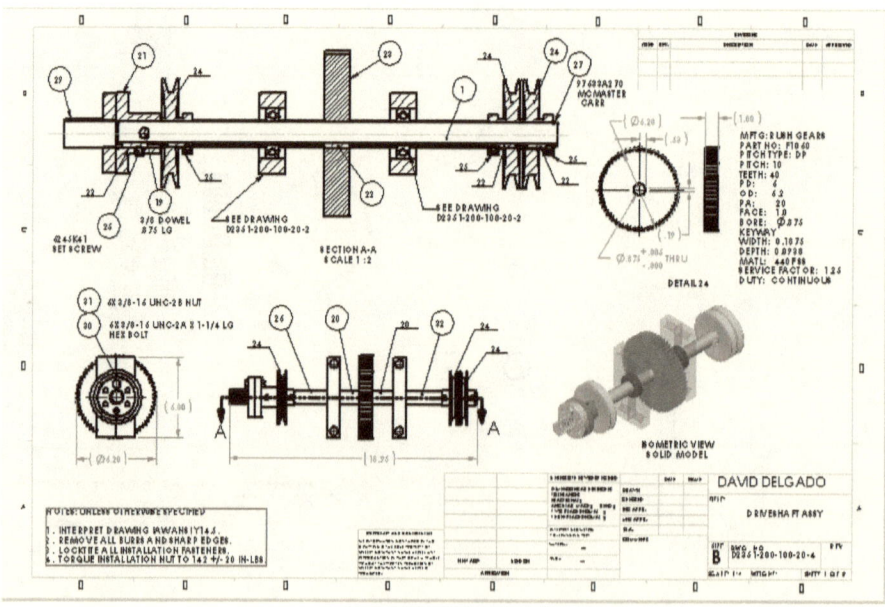

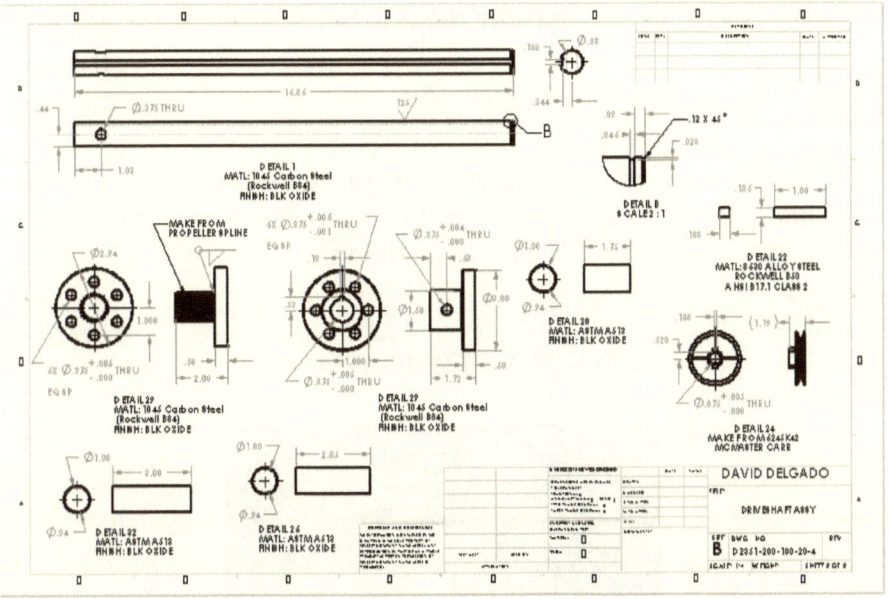

About the Author

Dave Delgado started two years studing Automotive classes in high school.   Finally retiring as Chief Engineer with Process Fab Inc., Santa Fe, California

https://davedelgado.webs.com/

Inmate

www.ingramcontent.com/pod-product-compliance
Lightning Source LLC
Chambersburg PA
CBHW020320290526
45785CB00007B/2855